MARATHONS
OF THE WORLD

First edition for North America published in 2013
by Barron's Educational Series, Inc.

Published in the United Kingdom by New Holland Publishers (UK) Ltd
Copyright © 2012 text and illustrations
London • Cape Town • Sydney • Auckland
www.newhollandpublishers.com

Garfield House, 86–88 Edgware Road
London W2 2EA, UK

Wembley Square, Solan Street, Gardens
Cape Town 8000, South Africa

Unit 1, 66 Gibbes Street, Chatswood
New South Wales 2067, Australia

218 Lake Road, Northcote
Auckland, New Zealand

All inquiries should be addressed to:
Barron's Educational Series, Inc.
250 Wireless Boulevard
Hauppauge, NY 11788
www.barronseduc.com

Library of Congress Control Number: 2012954036

ISBN: 978-0-7641-6609-9

Publishing Director Lliane Clarke
Publisher Guy Hobbs
Designer Paul Wright
Production Manager Marion Storz
Cartographer Bill Smuts

Printed and bound in China by Toppan Leefung Printing Ltd
9 8 7 6 5 4 3 2 1

PICTURE CREDITS
Alamy: page 146, 147; Corbis: page 46–47; Getty Images: page 25;
Shutterstock: page 17, 76–77, 93, 105, 106, 107, 111, 112, 113, 114,
129, 130, 131, 132, 133, 135

The publishers would like to thank all of the marathon organizers for
generously supplying images for use in this publication, specifically
the organizers of Stockholm, Chicago and the Reggae marathons.
Thanks to Mike King for the Antarctic images, and Wild Frontiers for
the Kilimanjaro pictures.

Disclaimer
Although the marathon details provided here are thought to be
accurate at the time of going to press, the information regarding
marathon events and their organizers is liable to change. If you are
planning to run a marathon check the organizer's website regularly to
ensure you comply with their entry requirements.

MARATHONS
OF THE WORLD

Hugh Jones and
Alexander James

BARRON'S

Contents | From East to West

Introduction

Selecting only 50 races to be included in this book was a harder task than it might seem. There are now so many marathons in almost every country and territory of the world – from the North Pole and Antarctica to the Sahara Desert, as well as on islands so small that the organizers struggle to set out a route of 26.2 miles (42.2 km). The sheer variety on offer dazzles the imagination.

It is hard to believe that the first marathon race (aside from that of the ancient legend) was held little more than a century ago, and the sort of popular running event that we take for granted today only started to emerge in the late 1970s. The Greek legend recounts the story of Pheidippides, a messenger who was sent from the battlefield of Marathon to Athens to deliver news of victory over the Persian army. Exhausted, he expired on arrival, having run a distance now thought to be farther than the modern marathon. The story's romantic appeal inspired Michel Breal, a renowned philologist, to prevail upon his friend Baron Pierre de Coubertin, the founder of the Modern Olympic Games, to include a long-distance race from Marathon to Athens in the inaugural Olympic Games in Greece in the summer of 1896.

Above: Bridges feature in many marathons and offer a spectacular sight from above.

Left: The Rome Marathon is a world-class event with competitors from around the world running through the city.

The first marathon was actually a trial race held a few months before in April 1896, and over the same course. The defining Olympic race played out dramatically and promoters immediately sought to emulate it, primarily in Europe and North America.

The Boston Marathon was born the following year. It has proven to be the most resilient, maintaining continuity through both world wars and the Great Depression and, after a few shaky years in the 1980s, reinventing itself to follow a more popular formula. In England the Polytechnic Marathon (the "Poly"), from Windsor to Chiswick, started in 1909, following the 1908 London Olympic Marathon, and was held over a similar course. Many world records were set on this course in the 1950s and 1960s, but the race petered out in the 1990s as the new generation of big-city marathons took over.

The "popular formula" of marathon running was conceived by Fred Lebow, a New Yorker and avid runner, in a fortuitous confluence of circumstances – the running world's "Eureka" moment. Prior to this date marathons were typically run by a band of elite, usually male, runners who had to complete the course in fast times or were asked to withdraw from the race. Lebow, who had established the New York Marathon in 1970 as a four-lap race within the confines of Central Park, followed up on a suggestion from local distance-runner Ted Corbett to make the race "citywide"

Above: Clean air and spectacular scenery are just two of the attractions for the Jungfrau Marathon in Switzerland.

in its appeal. City Hall seized upon the idea, but misinterpreted it as a proposal to run the race through all five boroughs of the city to celebrate the American bicentennial in 1976. Consequently, the field had grown from 534 starters in 1975 to 2,090 participants in just one year. The spectacle it presented enthused enough people to fuel rapid growth, and in 1980, 14,000 runners entered the race.

Several of the races included in this book were a direct outgrowth of the New York experience. Even those already in existence, like Berlin, cashed in on the move to citywide marathon courses. Others, like Stockholm, Barcelona, and London, were set up by those who had been impressed by New York and realized that it was an event waiting to happen in other cities of the world.

The "running boom" as it became known, which started with New York in the late 1970s, caught on in Europe in the early 1980s.

In Japan, marathons were already firmly embedded in the public's awareness: the elite Japanese Fukuoka Marathon had taken over from England's "Poly" as the place to set world records in the late 1960s. For most Japanese, however, it remained a spectator sport as the field remained closed to all but elite runners. Many Japanese runners traveled abroad to find big-city marathons in which they could take part. Pressure built upon Japanese race organizers to open up their events to mass participation. Finally, after long, hard scrutiny of races elsewhere and careful planning, they did just this in 2007 and met with instant success.

By contrast, marathon running was almost unknown in India when the Mumbai Marathon was launched in 2003. By that date marathons had already become far more than just running events and featured carnival aspects including outlandish costumes and huge charity fundraising. Mumbai capitalized on this, with supporting events that attracted corporate advertising, cricketing heroes, and Bollywood stars. Running, and the Mumbai Marathon with it, became an aspirational pursuit for tens of thousands of people.

Marathons have conquered the world's big cities, and they are increasingly reaching far more remote locations, specifically aimed at attracting tourist runners. While many of the big-city marathons entice significant numbers of foreigners and contribute heavily to the local economy as a result, others – like the Great Wall Marathon in China – attract an almost exclusively tourist clientele. The Australian Outback Marathon, near Uluru, does the same, even though the overwhelming majority of runners are Australians. The attraction is obvious – if you are adventurous enough to run a marathon, the idea of doing it in an appealing location gives an extra incentive.

I came to marathon running when it was an elite performance sport. People taking up running since the 1980s have done so mainly to participate rather than compete. The two are hardly exclusive of each other but bring different perspectives. As a career marathon runner, I ran where I could perform best and where the performance would count for most. That was why I ran in New York, Tokyo, London, Chicago, and Beijing, not in the race that offered the most challenging or beautiful course or the most exotic location, but on a fast course in which I could excel. All world records have been set in big-budget races – since these are the events that attract the professional runners. New York was the first such event, paying out large prize money.

Most runners with an eye on the clock will target a "fast" course at some point, in order to obtain the much discussed "personal best" time, but they may also be attracted to races that hold out the promise of a memorably different experience. For me, the one that offered a completely different experience was the Sahara Marathon. Like some of the other adventure races in this book, such as the Great Wall Marathon or the North Pole Marathon, runners meet up even before arriving at the race. Typically a rapport develops that is only strengthened as the race approaches, with participants sharing accommodation within the homes of the Sahrawi refugees and experiencing the place in a profound way.

Wherever you run, running a marathon allows a deeper sense of participation within a city or country than is open to a visitor with a more casual itinerary, whether at home or abroad. For the social runner, the challenge of running such a long distance will always hold special memories whatever the location. The chance to participate in a race at the same time as the world's elite is appealing: the marathon is the only event where the masses can be on the same course, at the same time, as the best in the world.

Marathons bring a sense of purpose, too, as you set out on a journey and see it through to the finish. My victory in the second London

Above: The appeal of many marathons for tourists is the opportunity to visit exotic towns and cities.

Right: Millennium Park, a landmark of the Chicago Marathon.

Marathon, back in 1982, brought an overwhelming sense of relief. I thought I could do it – other people also seemed to think so – but it was only crossing the finish line that made it reality. Most marathon experiences will be less stark than that, and perhaps may be better appreciated and more enjoyable if the runner's concentration is focused on the taking part rather than the end result. For many first-time runners, marathon day may be the end of the journey, preceded by months of mental and physical preparation, training schedules, and self-discipline so that the day might be better enjoyed and injury-free. For seasoned runners, who know what their bodies are capable of, achieving a faster marathon time might be the catalyst for entering a race. Whether your finish time is 2½ or 6 hours, the sense of achievement at completing a personal challenge, or knocking minutes or seconds off your time, can be immense.

The races described in this book offer a huge variety of different experiences. The world is out there waiting for you, and as a marathon runner you are well placed to conquer it. Marathon running involves commitment and a sense of purpose, and it will be rewarding in whatever circumstances it is realized. Look through these pages for a glimpse of the magical places to which it can transport you.

Hugh Jones

Above: The runners in the Sahara Marathon stay as guests in the refugee camps, focusing attention on the plight of the Sahrawi and promoting better understanding.

Auckland Marathon | New Zealand

For most foreign runners the Auckland Marathon is a very long way away, but the event offers something for everyone – with a family run; a 3-mile (5 km) race; and quarter, half, and full marathons all being staged at the same time. Only the marathon and half marathon cross the Auckland Harbor Bridge, which is the big feature of the course.

The marathon was founded by the YMCA Marathon Club in 1994 as two laps along the Tamaki Drive Waterfront to the east of the city center. Only when the course was changed to include the Harbor Bridge and the city center did it generate the international profile the organizers sought. Numbers grew and now stand at 14,000, with just over half of them women. Of those, 3,000 entries are for the marathon, making it a fairly low-key event when compared with some of the larger marathons. There is an intimate feel to the race that is only partly to do with the limited numbers.

Before dawn, runners board a flotilla of chartered ferries to take them from the city center across Waitemata Harbor to the start line in Devonport on the north shore. The early start is a sensible solution to the logistical problem of how to get runners from one side of the bridge to the other in the limited time available; the bridge has to be reopened to general traffic at 9:45 am, come what may. Marathon runners set off at 6:10 am and the half marathoners follow at 7:00 am, giving them a generous cutoff time to reach the the crucial 8-mile (13 km) point at which they ascend onto the bridge – if they are not there in time they are turned away.

From the start at Torpedo Bay, runners go north on the peninsular turning onto the mainland proper at Takapuna, 5 miles (8 km) into the race. They then head south toward the bridge. Descending through Point Erin Park, runners go eastbound along the waterfront to approach the city center. Before getting there, half marathon runners turn into Victoria Park to finish, but marathon runners bypass the center by hugging the wharf to emerge on a causeway heading out to a turning point at 18½ miles (30 km).

Runners press on to the causeway, which the quarter marathon runners, who began outside Victoria Park and turned here for their return to the finish, have cleared by the time the marathon runners arrive. The wealthy waterfront suburbs start from here, and marathon runners can enjoy the spectacular harbor views as they press on for another 3 miles (5 km) to the turning point at St. Helier Bay.

Retracing the third quarter of the route in reverse to the Victoria Park finish, the "Party in the Park" welcomes weary finishers with bands, entertainment, and a plethora of hospitality tents provided for the estimated 38,000 people attending the celebrations. It is an experience far removed from the peaceful early morning ferry ride across the harbor, but a suitably ebullient end to a hard race. The average time for the course is an impressive 4½ hours, with most runners home while the day is still young.

Right: The Sky Tower looms in the background, an iconic landmark visible throughout the race.

Below: The bridge marks the end of the hilly section of the race, though the incline onto it is the steepest of all.

RACE DETAILS

WHEN? October
WHEN TO APPLY: July
HOW MANY TAKE PART? 15,000
DIFFICULTY RATING: 6/10
SPECIAL CONSIDERATIONS: Hilly at the start but largely flat afterwards. The course can be windy, so keep hydrated.

CONTACT: Adidas Auckland Marathon
M129, Private Bag 300987
Albany
Auckland, New Zealand
☎ +64 (0)9 415 0617
✉ racedirector@aucklandmarathon.co.nz
▭ www.aucklandmarathon.co.nz

Sydney Marathon | Australia

The Olympic Games hosted by Sydney in 2000 allowed Australia to project its sport-friendly environment to a watching world. One Olympic legacy that resulted is the Blackmore's Festival of Running Sydney Marathon.

The Sydney Marathon – for short – is the only event arising from the 2000 Olympics that is open to the public. From the first staging it attracted 7,500 runners. The numbers have been growing ever since, and it is now one of the most popular sporting events in Australia. The appeal is obvious – you get to run across the iconic Sydney Harbor Bridge and gaze down on the Harbor, the Opera House, and the Botanical Gardens as you go.

The finish is at the World Heritage Site of Sydney Opera House, and the great thing about this inclusive running festival is that you get all these impressive sights no matter which running option you choose out of the marathon, the half marathon, the 5½-mile (9 km) bridge run, and the 2½-mile (4 km) family fun run, all of which are staged at the same event. The organizers go to great and varied lengths to live up to their slogan, "The run that's fun for everyone." The family fun run route follows a direct track to the Opera House, the bridge run makes a lap out of it, and the marathon and half marathon routes twist around the city center in intricate webs that feature many hairpin turns. The marathon makes up the required distance by leading runners on a continuously sinuous route to the southeast of the city center, in and around Centennial Park. The course is undulating but includes several long, flat sections. The weather is generally 66–70°F (19–21°C), with the occasional welcome breeze to help you cool off.

The idea of a running festival, rather than a race, hinges on the idea of making it easy and fun for everyone to take part in one of the events on offer. The organizers have clearly achieved this goal, as a total of 30,000 people hit the streets of Sydney, even if some of them do end up walking the entire course.

WHILE YOU'RE THERE

You'll never tire of looking at the beauty of **Sydney Harbor** and its skyline, comprising the Opera House and bridge – a great way to see it is from the water by taking one of the many ferries that leave the harbor.
Keep on the watery track by feasting on the fish market offerings in **Pyrmont**. Or take your fresh food to **Bondi** or **Coogee Beach** and spark up a barbecue.

Right: The iconic sights of the city are visible in the Sydney Marathon.

RACE DETAILS

WHEN? September
WHEN TO APPLY: June
HOW MANY TAKE PART? 30,000
DIFFICULTY RATING: 7/10
SPECIAL CONSIDERATIONS: The course is undulating. Bring your own energy gels.

CONTACT:
Sydney Running Festival
Level 2, 5 Queen St
Chippendale
NSW, Australia
☎ +61 2 9282 0400
✉ info@sydneyrunningfestival.org
🖥 www.sydneyrunningfestival.com.au

Australian Outback Marathon | Australia

The Australian Outback's most identifiable landmark, Uluru, otherwise known as Ayers Rock, is a spiritual center for the indigenous Aborigines of Australia. Those who run in the presence of its red glow say it is a life-transforming experience.

Running this event allows you to see at close quarters the Central Australian "red earth" in a way that is almost impossible as a private individual. That is because the marathon, half marathon, 6¾-mile (11 km) and 3¾-mile (6 km) events take place on private land that is not only inaccessible to visitors but is also off-limits to those who live and work in Yulara town and the surrounding area.

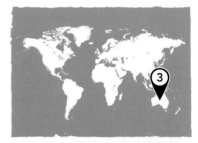

3

WHILE YOU'RE THERE

There is a **celebration dinner** as part of the marathon, held outdoors at a private site. Champagne and canapés are served upon arrival, and guests are serenaded by the marathon's own **didgeridoo player** while the sun sets over Uluru. By night find **an astronomer** onsite to point out the constellations, as there is absolutely no atmospheric pollution to dim the glow of the night sky. See: www.australiasoutback.com.

The Australian Outback Marathon was conceived during a visit to Uluru in 2004 by two race visionaries, Mari-Mar and Michael Walton. Both were working on behalf of an agency called Travelling Fit. Not having been to Uluru before, they were in awe of the area and knew that it would be the perfect location for a running event. After several years of work on the idea was done, permissions were finally granted in 2008, and the Australian Outback Marathon was born.

The amazing landscape of Uluru and Kata Tjuta (a significant group of rock formations, locally called the Olgas) allows runners and spectators alike to appreciate views of these World Heritage–listed Sites from almost every part of the course. It is, however, only when you see these monolithic forms from a distance that you get a real sense of how large and majestic they are. With so few spectators along the course, runners get the feeling that they are at one with the spirit of the Australian Outback.

There are approximately 1¼ miles (2 km) of sealed roads on the course as well as an additional 1¼ miles (2 km) of unsealed but graded roads, and despite the dust and dirt, the route generally offers a firm footing. As the area was once an ancient seabed, the course is flat, but there are a few sand dunes to navigate that enliven the run, and the views from the top are breathtaking.

Previous page: Spectacular countryside and a small field are two very appealing aspects of this course.

Above: Jogging in the "red center," as this part of the vast Outback is known, almost feels like you are on a different planet.

Right: The tracks and trails of the marathon course are made up of the famous red earth that surround the Ayers Rock Resort.

RACE DETAILS

WHEN? July
WHEN TO APPLY: February
HOW MANY TAKE PART? 2,000
DIFFICULTY RATING: 6/10
SPECIAL CONSIDERATIONS: Hot and
dry terrain as you'd expect from this part
of the planet; an unpredictable landscape
requires endurance and adaptability.

CONTACT:
Travelling Fit
Level 1, Suite 5
66 Terrigal Espalanade
Terrigal, NSW, Australia
☎ +61 2 4385 2455 (international)
✉ sales@australianoutbackmarathon.com
🖥 www.australianoutbackmarathon.com

Tokyo Marathon | Japan

Japan is one of the foremost countries of the world when it comes to marathons. The country's Olympic marathon record, from 1936 to the present, is second to none. The key to this has been an unrelenting concentration on elite performance. Marathons staged in Japan have traditionally been for restricted fields of a few dozen elite men or women – with separate races for each on the championship model. Road space was freed up for these events by using a "rolling closure," and if runners did not stay on schedule to finish in under 2½ or 3 hours, then they were "retired" into the sweep vehicle.

If you were an ordinary Japanese citizen and you wanted to take part in a marathon, your best chance was to jump on a plane and go to Honolulu, Hawaii, to run in a race where the field comprised mainly other Japanese runners. But that all changed with the advent of the first mass marathon in Japan, the 2007 Tokyo Marathon. Since 1981 Japanese marathons had subscribed to the elite model described above, but after minutely observing mass marathons in the rest of the world and spending years planning their groundbreaking event, the Tokyo Marathon took the world by storm.

The 2007 race itself was a washout, as it rained heavily for the duration. Yet such is the affinity the Japanese have for marathon running that it did not dampen their spirit. That first event was swamped by eager entrants, and now two or three times as many people apply for places as there are spaces. There is no indication that the Japanese love affair with marathon running is anywhere near over, as many of Japan's main cities are following Tokyo's example and converting their events to the popular model (among them Osaka, Kyoto, Nagoya, and Kobe).

It is the city's dedication to holding this event that defines the atmosphere – support is strong and public enthusiasm has always been there, even when the crowds at the roadside were encouraging national heroes rather than their nearest and dearest. Those who were not on the roadside were watching it on TV – Japan has the highest television-viewing figures for a marathon anywhere recorded.

WHILE YOU'RE THERE

Tokyo has the most populated landscape in the world, and its high-tech construction never fails to amaze.

Among the historic sites you should see are the **temples of Asakusa,** the **Imperial Palace,** and the **Meiji Shrine.**

To get a grasp of this metropolis, go to the top of the **Tokyo Metropolitan Government Building,** where you can benefit from a free view of the city. See: www.seejapan.co.uk

Right: Marathon running is a significant sport in Japan, where the events receive plenty of popular support.

RACE DETAILS

WHEN? February
WHEN TO APPLY: One year in advance
HOW MANY TAKE PART? 35,000
DIFFICULTY RATING: 4/10
SPECIAL CONSIDERATIONS: Fast and flat course that is surprisingly free of congestion. Be prepared for unpredictable weather and wind.

CONTACT:
KNT Tokyo Marathon Entry Desk
Kinki Nippon Tourist Co, Ltd (KNT)
Global Business Management Branch
Sumitomo-shoji kanda -Izumi-cho Bldg
12F,1–13 Kanda-Izumi-cho, Chiyoda-ku
Tokyo 101-0024, Japan

☎ +813 6891 9600
🖳 www.tokyo42195.org

The start gun fires at the Tokyo Metropolitan Government Building, setting runners off on a downhill gradient toward the city's Yasukuni Shrine, before taking a turn past the Imperial Palace and onward to Hibiya Park. Marathon day is the only time when these key landmarks are free of traffic, and that alone is worth celebrating. The distance from 7–20 miles (11–32 km) is relatively flat, but the test comes in the last quarter of the race, as runners must find the energy to ascend three bridges.

Runners come, under their own steam, from as many as 49 different countries, to a race that only a few years ago was by invitation only. Organizers want to see increasing international participation in the race, and it seems that they have many takers, all eager to experience the new developments in the world's most marathon-committed nation. Following the devastating earthquake and tsunami of 2011, future editions of the marathon will devote a percentage of profits to disaster relief.

Above: Shiba Park is a key landmark in the first section of the race and is generally well supported by the crowds.

Beijing Marathon | China

Just like the Chinese tiger economy itself, this sporting spectacle is evolving with the same rampant fervor. The Beijing Marathon has gone from a minority event to one that sparkles with the verve of a city happy to shout about itself.

In 1980, a national sports conference was held in Beijing, at which it was decided to use sport to connect with the rest of the world. The Beijing Marathon was founded the following year as part of this outreach policy and marked the birth of the marathon in China. A total of 80 elite male runners were invited to participate in that first race, though they were almost lost in the immensity of the Tiananmen Square start and finish area. Women weren't accepted until 1989, the same year that amateur runners were first admitted. Participation has now reached 30,000, with the field divided between the marathon, a half marathon, and a fun run.

The start and finish were moved from Tiananmen Square to the Workers' Stadium for many years, though the start is now back in Tiananmen Square, just as it was for the 2008 Olympic Games. Apart from the first couple of miles (a few kilometers), the city marathon course is quite different from the Olympic one.

WHILE YOU'RE THERE

October is one of the best times to visit the city of Beijing, and there is always a packed arts program at the **National Theater**.

It is also the season to see the lotus flower in full glory, as well as the rich reds of the maple leaf. There is even a Maple Leaf Festival in the western reaches of Beijing at **Xiangshan**.

For some nighttime revelry the best nightlife spots are **Houhai Bar Street** and Sanlitun Bar Street.

Left: Beijing puts on a spectacle for the world to watch on marathon day.

From Tiananmen Square, the world's largest city-center square that can hold up to a million people, runners file past the Great Hall of the People, the Monument to the People's Heroes, the Chairman Mao Memorial Hall, and the gate to the Imperial Palace, or "Forbidden City." This impressive grouping of sights is all in the first thousand feet approximately (a few hundred meters), then followed by long, straight sections without much to see as the route loops through the western side of town.

Below: Tiananmen Square is synonymous with the imagery of China. It is here, in front of the portrait of Chairman Mao, where the marathon gets underway.

The National Museum of China and Zhongshan Park are the most prominent landmarks, until the runners reach the 2008 Olympic Stadium, known to the world as the Bird's Nest, with the Olympic Aquatic Center alongside it.

The Marathon is held every year on the third Sunday in October during Beijing's golden autumn, when it is dry and cool and the city is at its very best.

RACE DETAILS

WHEN? October
WHEN TO APPLY: By July
HOW MANY TAKE PART? 30,000
DIFFICULTY RATING: 5/10
SPECIAL CONSIDERATIONS: It is a race you run for the experience, not the scenery. Tiananmen Square is subject to tight security, so try and arrive one hour before the start time. Traffic can be difficult.

CONTACT:

✉ oc@beijingmarathon.com
🖥 wwwbeijingmarathon.com

The Great Wall Marathon | China

If running a marathon isn't a big enough test, then try doing it along the Great Wall of China. Taking on the 5,164 steps of this world-famous structure is one of the biggest challenges a runner can face.

Many have called the Great Wall Marathon the hardest marathon in the world. But the race is equally one of the most picturesque, offering the thrill of competing on top of one the world's great landmarks.

Built on a mountain range, the wall rises and drops dramatically and offers consistently superb views. The section of the route run along the wall is just over 2 miles (3.5 km) long, with the rest on asphalt roads through nearby villages.

RACE DETAILS

WHEN? May
WHEN TO APPLY: A year in advance due to small capacity
HOW MANY TAKE PART? 2,000
DIFFICULTY RATING: 8/10
SPECIAL CONSIDERATIONS: Supreme stamina required as you don't just run past the wall, but also run up it. Plenty of water is provided. Bring your own gels if you want them.

CONTACT:
The Great Wall Marathon, Head Office
Room 1201, Unit 2, Bld A
Fenghuahaojing
6 Guang'anmennel Street
Beijing 100053, China
☎ +86 10 6355 2521
✉ gwm-bookings@263.net.cn
🖳 www.great-wall-marathon.com/

6

WHILE YOU'RE THERE

The engineering feat of the Great Wall is worth another look after the run. One of the best spots to see it is at **Mutianyu**, which is less crowded and surrounded by greenery. The wall stretches through the spectacular wildlife habitats, offering the lucky few an opportunity to spot the **Siberian tiger**, the **giant panda**, **black bears**, and the **Sitka deer**, which all live along the length of the wall. See: www.cnto.org.uk

The surrounding area is just as fascinating as the Great Wall itself. Huangyaguan, in Tianjin Province, is a remote area and, with the Great Wall as an astonishing backdrop, the route goes past rice fields and farmland and through small Chinese villages. These are remnants of a fast-disappearing China, a district yet to benefit from the building boom and growing economy of the Chinese capital, which is a three-hour drive away.

Runners should not expect large crowds of spectators, but the local villagers always turn out in force. Children in particular throng the course, offering heartening support to the runners. The configuration of the course allows family members and friends to gather at the start and finish, to cheer runners home.

The first race, held in 1999, was intended to be a one-off adventure for a group of 300 Danish runners, but it was so well received that organizers decided to make it an annual event. The half marathon was added in 2001, and the 6-mile (10 km)

Previous page: Running on the Great Wall is one of life's incredible experiences.

Above: The Great Wall is the width of a marching army in places, but the surface is uneven and sloping in all directions, and this adds to the difficulty of the race.

Top right: The Great Wall Marathon is an endurance test at altitude as much as a marathon – not for the faint-hearted.

Bottom right: Dirt tracks make up more than half of the terrain of the marathon and are usually lined with local well-wishers.

and 3-mile (5 km) distances in 2004. Numbers have grown steadily from just under 100 runners in 2000 to more than 1,700 10 years later. Logistics in such a remote area and the need to limit numbers on the wall itself make it likely that organizers will cap the field at 2,000. Temperatures are usually around 68–77°F (20–25°C), but there have been years when they have reached 95°F (35°C). A low of 61°F (16°C) was recorded in 2008. Rain is unusual at the time of the race.

The steps on the Great Wall are the major challenge, especially as they are steep, irregular, and uneven. The rest of the route is also testing, as the gravel and dirt roads wind through hilly farmland and villages. This marathon is not one for fast times, and runners would not want to spend much time looking at their watch when there is so much else around to take in. This run offers a unique and life-enhancing experience that is not available from more conventional organized tours to visit the Great Wall.

Siberian International Marathon | Russia

In this part of western Siberia, this race is awaited with the same anticipation as a national holiday. So closely does the marathon touch the Siberian soul that a statue, "The Flying Marathoner," was erected in the heart of the city as a reminder to those who might otherwise miss the event. Come race day it is adorned with the names of the participants who have come to run.

As soon as the city of Omsk opened its doors to visitors in 1990, an international marathon was organized to mark this historic event. More than 40 nationalities come from far-flung corners of the globe to take part each year and are greeted with open arms. It is something locals look forward to, and during the buildup, advertisements abound with the marathon logos. The city's media approach a frenzy in their constant chatter about the race events. All this builds excitement and anticipation. On race day the full cross-section of Omsk society turns out in force.

With the most "continental" of climates – being a few thousand miles (several thousand kilometers) from the nearest ocean – Omsk is bone-chillingly cold in winter but on race day basks in the early August sunshine. For the last 10 years the average temperature on marathon day has been 71–77°F (22–25°C).

The start is heralded by church bells ringing at the 17th-century Cathedral of the Assumption, outside which the race begins and ends. The first part of the course takes runners through the 19th-century part of town, built at a time when the Tsarist Empire was still consolidating its grip on its sub-Asiatic hinterland. Runners run out and back along the birch-lined embankments of the impressively broad Irtysh River. The second half of the course runs through the industrial part of the city, including the largest oil refinery in Russia.

Spectators who don't find viewing space at the start have plenty of opportunity to intercept the runners at other points along the course. People turn out in force to support runners in all possible ways – only in Omsk will you be offered cranberry water and homemade pies as you run.

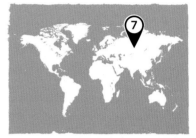

WHILE YOU'RE THERE

The city center around **Lyubinsky Prospekt** is best explored on foot as the stomping ground of Russia's great literary giant Dostoevsky. The historical part of town is centered here, near the **Om** and **Irtysh Rivers**. It is lined with century-old buildings of former merchant salons, **grand residences, and churches**. Omsk was a center for the Trans-Siberian Railway, which brought great affluence in the early 20th century.

Right: The Siberian Marathon takes place at the start of a week of national festivities and is well supported by local people in the city.

The closing ceremony is treated as seriously as at the Olympic Games. Russian sports journalist Boris Prokopiev, making a direct comparison, described it as "bright, colorful, gorgeous; a sports performance lasting hours and incorporating effects like waterfalls of balloons and fireworks as the athletes stand proudly on the rostrum."

RACE DETAILS

WHEN? August
WHEN TO APPLY: December of the year before
HOW MANY TAKE PART? 1,300
DIFFICULTY RATING: 7/10
SPECIAL CONSIDERATIONS: The weather is likely to be extreme and can sometimes hit 95–104°F (35–40°C). A largely flat course on asphalt.

CONTACT:
Siberian International Marathon (SIM)
Pevtsova str. 1,
644099, Omsk, Russia
☎ +7 495 646 8368
✉ info@russianmarathons.com
🖥 www.russianmarathons.com

Mumbai Marathon | India

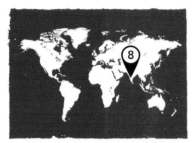

WHILE YOU'RE THERE

Just a day in the congested city might leave you wanting to escape to find some fresher air. Take a ferry near the **Gate of India** landmark to **Elephant Island** to see ancient temples carved into caves.

One of the best treats you can give yourself after the marathon is to take afternoon tea at the **Leela Hotel** (www.theleela.com), one of India's most affordable lavish hotels.

Or if you have more than a few days to spare, take the train to sunny **Goa**, and enjoy its many beaches.

Right: Helicopters are used to capture footage that is shown around the world.

Far right: This is a marathon with plenty of views to occupy the runners' attention.

The Mumbai Marathon was born with a bang in 2004 and launched with all the razzmatazz you would expect of a Bollywood blockbuster. Hyped in the newspapers daily for the month before the marathon, street billboards bellowed the message and a laser show projected images onto the side of the Air India building on Marine Drive – visible to all for miles around. Would this fledgling event collapse under the weight of its own expectation, especially as Indian participants were nowhere to be seen?

But the Mumbai Marathon is a festival and a celebration – it may be spearheaded by top-class international runners, but everyone wants a piece of the action. The organizers appreciated this from the start, knowing that there was no room for half measures, and fought a long, hard battle with sometimes reluctant officials to clear a space for the marathon on Mumbai's crowded streets. With some visionary help from people in high places, the show got on the road after only one year of preparing the ground.

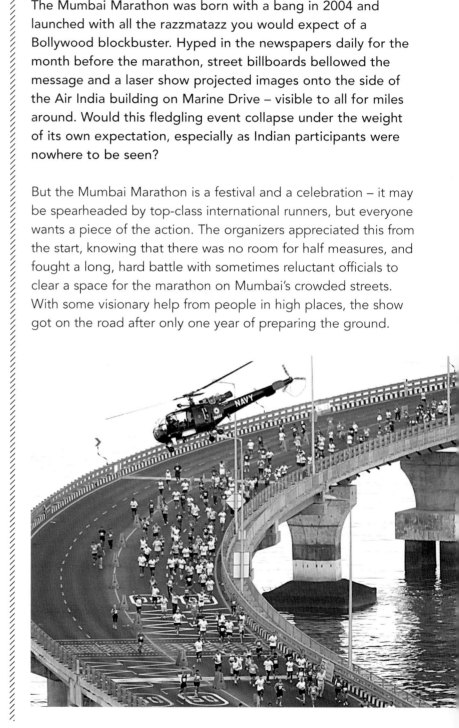

RACE DETAILS

WHEN? January
WHEN TO APPLY: July to August of the previous year
HOW MANY TAKE PART? 38,400
DIFFICULTY RATING: 7/10
SPECIAL CONSIDERATIONS: This marathon is one for the experienced runner rather than a first-timer. Water stations are plentiful. Hot and humid temperatures. The course is congested in the early stages and at the finish.

CONTACT:
Procam International
14, St. James Court, Marine Drive,
Mumbai - 400020, India
☎ +91 22 4202 0200
✉ scmm@procam.in
🖥 www.procamrunning.in

Mumbai permanently buzzes with swarms of cars, trucks, taxis, and bikes, with the occasional cow weaving its way through the urban mayhem. That is just on a quiet day. Marathon day brings a completely different feel, as the roads are cleared to make way for a spectacle that brings this city together. Everyone, from Bollywood stars and heavyweight corporate players to juice wallahs and street urchins, are either watching or taking part in a display of solidarity for an international event that is beamed across the world.

Never was this more evident than on January 18, 2009, when the race went ahead just seven weeks after the terrorist attacks that attempted to cripple the city. The marathon was a statement of the collective will of its citizens, expressing both their strong spirit and their resolve.

As a runner you'll be swept up in the tide of marathon fever come race day. More than 1,000 volunteers, private security guards, and 800 police secure the course, which goes out and back, taking in a loop of Mumbai's new addition to the urban landscape – the 2½-mile (4 km) Bandra-Worli Sealink, which, although devoid of spectators, offers impressive panoramas of the city.

Largely because of the Mumbai Marathon, running has become fashionable among the Bollywood set, and this is reflected in the aspirational demographic among the tens of thousands of entrants in the marathon (2,800), half marathon (11,000) and 3¾-mile (6 km) "Dream Run" (22,500). This is all despite the climate, which is not conducive to fast running, although the heat is offset somewhat by the early 5:15 am marathon start.

Invited elite runners have recorded surprisingly fast times – men under 2:10 and women 2:26. Indian athletes habitually run their fastest times in the race, spurred on by the occasion and the illustrious competition.

The Mumbai Marathon, with its inclusive and international spirit, is not just a race, but a vision of a new India.

Left: The elite runners in any marathon field are a sight to behold.

RACE DETAILS

WHEN? February
WHEN TO APPLY: June of the year before
HOW MANY TAKE PART? 5,000
DIFFICULTY RATING: 8/10
SPECIAL CONSIDERATIONS: There are
long stretches of uphill running. Things can
get hot, humid and dusty, often reaching
more than 86°F (30°C), but there is plenty
of shade as well as water stations. Traffic
and exhaust fumes can be an issue.

CONTACT:
Wild Frontiers (Pty) Ltd
PO Box 844
Halfway House 1685
South Africa
☎ +27 011 702 2035
✉ reservations@wildfrontiers.com
🖥 www.kilimanjaromarathon.com

Kilimanjaro Marathon | Tanzania

Climbing Mount Kilimanjaro features on more than a few people's ultimate wish list of things to do before they die. Running the Kilimanjaro Marathon provides a taste of the same adventure, taking the runner up as far as the lower slopes of the world's highest "free-standing" mountain.

Mount Kilimanjaro, at just short of 19,700 ft (6,000 m), is Africa's highest mountain. Glaciers flow down from the summit, and the sheer presence of this huge mountain dominates the northern part of Tanzania for miles around. An icon in Africa, "Kili" as she is affectionately known is one of the sights everyone should see at least once up close.

WHILE YOU'RE THERE

If you have time, combine some of the highlights of Africa with your trip to Kilimanjaro. Visit the **Ngorongoro Crater**, a UNESCO World Heritage Site, and the only place in the world that protects the landscape for wildlife while allowing humans to inhabit the land. Equally rewarding and closer is the **Serengeti National Park**. Others may decide to relax on the **beaches of Zanzibar**. Just 25 miles (40 km) from Tanzania's coast, this beautiful island has dazzling white beaches and coral reefs.

The route that awaits both social runners and serious athletes is challenging. The marathon starts in Moshi Stadium and takes the road toward Dar-es-Salaam for approximately 5 miles (8–9 km) on a route that is reassuringly flat. Runners turn around, heading back toward the start before turning off to make a loop toward the mountain. The steady ascent toward the village of Mweka begins here. The climb is unrelenting but gradual, and with Kilimanjaro towering above and local villagers who come out to cheer, morale remains high. You reach the turnaround point at 20 miles (32 km), and the last section is a fast downhill run to the stadium from where you began. Water tables and the odd shower to keep the runners refreshed and cool are dotted along the entire route.

Previous page: The start of the race is well supported with a party atmosphere as the athletes ready themselves for the course ahead.

Above: As its growing popularity attests, running a marathon under the watchful eye of Mount Kilimanjaro is an experience that any runner will treasure.

Right: This marathon field is relatively small but well supported.

The scenery encapsulates Africa's traditional landscape and local life. It passes many small farms, villages, and banana and coffee plantations, as well as patches of forest. You get a real flavor of Africa as you run past the markets, shops, and shebeens of Moshi. Local children often run alongside, holding your hand as they cheer you on. The race provides a source of great excitement to the residents, who give ample vocal support. It is their presence, as much as that of the awe-inspiring mountain, that remains etched in your memory.

Kilimanjaro Marathon started as a small affair with only 500 runners and has since grown to involve almost 5,000, split between the marathon, half marathon, and fun run.

Safaricom Marathon | Kenya

Transplanting a marathon race into a safari park is an unmistakably Western idea, although nonetheless an interesting one. The race was founded in 2000, when there was nothing else like it anywhere on the continent. Safaricom, the region's telecom provider, has helped to drum up foreign interest in running in Africa and has used the marathon as a vehicle to improve awareness of living conditions for the local people. Since the inaugural race, more than $3 million has been generated for wildlife conservation, community development, and health and education projects all over Kenya.

The event takes in spectacular scenery – Mount Kenya lies to the south of the Lewa Wildlife Conservancy, the site of the run, and there are breathtaking views north toward Samburu National Reserve and Mount Ololokwe. The course is challenging – with no asphalt in sight. It is all on dirt roads that form an undulating 13-mile (21 km) lap within the reserve, across the open savannah, along riverbanks, and through acacia woodland before finishing close to Lewa's Park headquarters. Half marathon runners do one lap of the course, while full marathon runners do two.

The heavily protected 65,000-acre (26,000 hectare) wildlife sanctuary is home to more than 100 rhinos, herds of elephants, and a vast assortment of plains game including zebras, giraffes, and buffalo, so you will never be far away from the wildlife. The thrill of running this race is that you are on the animals' territory. A large and experienced team of armed rangers watch over the route, with two helicopters and a spotter plane in the air throughout the race. Water stations and first aid points are situated every 1½ miles (2.5 km) along the course. Medical support at the finish is provided by the African Medical Research Foundation (AMREF) and its Flying Doctor Service, the Kenya Red Cross, and local hospitals.

Spectators have access to the route at certain points, and the understandable restrictions make support all the more appreciated and effective for the runners. Apart from these few

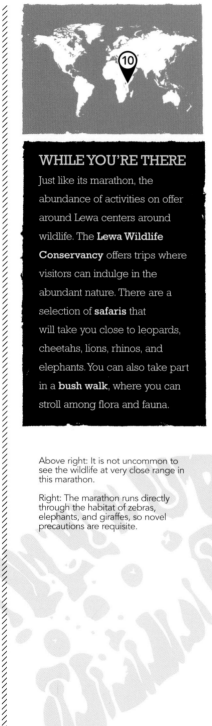

WHILE YOU'RE THERE

Just like its marathon, the abundance of activities on offer around Lewa centers around wildlife. The **Lewa Wildlife Conservancy** offers trips where visitors can indulge in the abundant nature. There are a selection of **safaris** that will take you close to leopards, cheetahs, lions, rhinos, and elephants. You can also take part in a **bush walk**, where you can stroll among flora and fauna.

Above right: It is not uncommon to see the wildlife at very close range in this marathon.

Right: The marathon runs directly through the habitat of zebras, elephants, and giraffes, so novel precautions are requisite.

points, runners sample the scenery in what must appear to be a vast wilderness away from civilization. Most runners and spectators spend the night before and after the race in Lewa in specially erected campsites within the conservation area. This gives the runners a chance to camp in the African bush and to see wildlife throughout the weekend.

The weather at the end of June, when the run is staged, is hot, with temperatures at midday around 86°F (30°C). Mornings and evenings are cool, with a strong breeze coming off the mountain. In addition, the race is run at an altitude of 5,580 feet (1,700 m), and this will have a definite restraining effect on the runners' pace.

RACE DETAILS

WHEN? June
WHEN TO APPLY: At least one year in advance
HOW MANY TAKE PART? 1,000
DIFFICULTY RATING: 8/10
SPECIAL CONSIDERATIONS: High elevations, hilly, sunny, and hot – it is not a race for the timid. Wildlife roams near the course, but guards are available to handle any risky situations. Water stations are placed every 1½ miles (2.5 km).

CONTACT:
Safaricom Marathon
c/o Kisima Ltd, Unit Kilo
Wilson Business Park
Wilson Airport
Nairopi, Kenya

✉ marathon@lewa.org
🖥 www.safaricom.co.ke

RACE DETAILS

WHEN? January
WHEN TO APPLY: June of the year before
HOW MANY TAKE PART? 1,500
DIFFICULTY RATING: 7/10
SPECIAL CONSIDERATIONS: The course can get congested and invaded by children asking for money.

CONTACT: Event Sports
1/4 Anwar El-Mofty St. (Area No.1)
Nasr City,
Cairo, Egypt
☎ +202 2260 69 30
✉ info@egyptianmarathon.net
🖥 www.egyptianmarathon.com

Egyptian Marathon | Luxor

Running in Egypt is an activity that is as old as the Pyramids: King Taharka, who reigned between 690 and 665 BC, established a 62-mile (100 km) race for his army. The Battle of Marathon in 490 BC was associated with the legend of a Greek soldier sent as a messenger from Marathon to Athens, a distance of around 28 miles (45 km). There is still a 62-mile (100 km) Pharaonic Race as well as the Egyptian Marathon itself, using the now standard marathon distance of 26.2 miles (42.2 km).

Luxor, the host city, offers mild to warm conditions in late January, when the run is scheduled, at a time when most of the Northern Hemisphere is suffering the chills of winter. The first event on the itinerary is a 2-mile (3.4 km) warm-up "breakfast run" starting at Luxor Temple and finishing at Karnak Temple, a massive complex that was the center of Theban civilization and evolved over 2,000 years. The participants keep the spirit of the past alive, and it is common to see them running in various Egyptian regalia, from Pharaonic costume to Cleopatra-style outfits.

The more serious racing starts the following day on the west bank of the Nile at 7:30 am, and with luck there will be a cool breeze wafting across the desert landscape. The race starts and finishes against the spectacular backdrop of Queen Hatshepsut's tomb – also justifiably known as the "Splendor of Splendors."

The four-lap route takes you to the entrance of the world-famous Valley of the Kings, which counts Tutankhamun's burial site among the many pharaohs entombed here. In benign conditions, because of the lack of shade, the first couple of laps on the wide and well-surfaced roads means that the run can be appreciated as a tour of an extraordinary outdoor museum. You pass the Temple of Ramses III and later the Colossi of Memnon. Beyond, there lies the timeless Egyptian countryside, with swathes of sugar cane, alfalfa, and date palms, creating a scene straight from a papyrus frieze, with runners as the focus of the composition.

Left: Running the Egyptian Marathon is like running through history, with ancient landmarks continually coming into view.

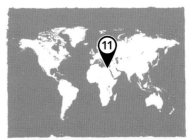

WHILE YOU'RE THERE

You don't have to go far to find some of the most awe-inspiring ancient temples on the planet once you're in the area, with the **Valley of the Kings** being a definite highlight.

There are three main areas to focus on once you're in town: the busy city center, the north-easterly village of **Karnak**, and also the many ancient remains of **Thebes**, located on the west bank of the world-famous River Nile. By night there is a guided light show around the relics. See: www.exodustravel.co.uk

"White Nights" Marathon | Russia

The name of the run is derived from the "white nights" that this part of northern Russia experiences in the height of summer. Almost 24 hours of sun lends a mysterious twilight to what many people call the country's most beautiful city – St. Petersburg, or Petersburg, to which it is more commonly referred. To run here provides an experience that is one of a kind.

Part of the challenge, however, is finding the essential information necessary to start in the first place. The race is not as well established as other events staged in major world cities and doesn't provide the same facilities that international runners might expect. So far, there are no official tour operators for the event, or even an online registration option. For many that come to run here, the absence of an organized administration is part of the charm, giving the same kind of rawness of spirit that old-style marathons had – but located in a major city.

Below: The "White Nights" Marathon was celebrated as part of St. Petersburg's tricentennial celebrations in 2003 and featured other fun runs.

RACE DETAILS

WHEN? Late June
WHEN TO APPLY: By January
HOW MANY TAKE PART? 1,100
DIFFICULTY RATING: 5/10
SPECIAL CONSIDERATIONS: The organization and setup is less structured than other world marathons. Advice and assistance is not too common. Prepare well in advance.

CONTACT:
White Nights Marathon
Office 11/2, Nevsky pr.32
St. Petersburg
Russia
☎ +812 312 90 15
✉ info@wnmarathon.ru
🖥 www.wnmarathon.ru

WHILE YOU'RE THERE

Take a day to explore what you might have missed on the run. **Peter and Paul Fortress** is the oldest existing building in St. Petersburg and was founded in 1703. Originally built by Peter the Great, it served as a prison until 1917. Famous prisoners included Dostoevsky, Alexander Lenin, and Gorky. **The Cathedral of Sts. Peter and Paul** is a must see with its legendary slender spire. Or go to **Petergof**, a collection of parks, palaces, and fountains that were once the summer residence of the tsars.

Those who make it here will discover Russia's greatest city awaiting them in all its glory. The fast marathon course follows river embankments and takes in historic landmarks such as the world-famous Hermitage museum, fabulous architecture, green spaces, and even the main shopping area. The start and finish takes place in the Palace Square.

Petersburg is young by European standards, founded just 300 years ago by Tsar Peter the Great. It became the Russian capital in 1712. The 300-day siege of Leningrad (as the city was known from 1924–91) occurred here during World War II, when almost three million civilians refused to surrender to their enemy, despite the hardships of famine and the bitter cold.

This marathon demands stoicism, but many find the challenge intensifies the experience. Rye bread, bananas, and bottled water are handed out at regularly positioned drink stations. If you want new-fangled sports drinks and gels, it is better to come prepared. Instead of clocks, you'll find there are strategically placed officials on hand to shout out your time.

Istanbul Marathon | Turkey

Istanbul is where Asia meets Europe. Its exclusive position provides the city with a unique selling point: this is the only race in the world in which you cross between two continents.

The incentive to stage a marathon here originally came from a sizable group of German runners who, after running a Nile Marathon, were looking for similar opportunities elsewhere. They provided 34 of the runners in that first event in 1979. Not many races are set up to serve a small group of interested foreign runners, but Istanbul's position as a continental crossing point meant that it could capitalize on the interest that foreign runners still continue to show in running in its symbolic location.

Runners complete only approximately a thousand feet (a few hundred meters) in Asia, as the race launches itself into Europe from the toll plaza on the Asian side of the Bosphorus Bridge. After the up-slope of the bridge, on the European side you drop down sharply, losing 100 yards (90 m) before reaching the Bosphorus after 3 miles (5 km). Thereafter, the course is nearly all flat until approximately the final half mile.

The course offers a combination of historic and scenic settings between the continents and the three strategic and historic waterways of the Bosphorus, the Golden Horn, and the Sea of Marmara. At the same time, the run takes a tour of more than 3,000 years of historical landmarks, during which three empires rose and fell.

Along the Bosphorus, giant Russian ships glide silently past, startlingly close, on their way from the Black Sea to the Mediterranean. On shore, the course takes you past the old and the new – from the 15th-century Rumelihisari fortress to the modern-day Galatasaray football stadium. After 6 miles (10 km) you pass below the 203-foot (62 m) high medieval stone Galata Tower, a Christian relic from pre-Ottoman times, before crossing the Galata Bridge over the Golden Horn.

Right: The Bosphorus Bridge represents the crossing point from Asia to Europe.

RACE DETAILS

WHEN? November
WHEN TO APPLY: February
HOW MANY TAKE PART? 4,500
DIFFICULTY RATING: 5/10
SPECIAL CONSIDERATIONS: Plan your journey to the starting point well. Sparse crowd support and toilet facilities. Weather can vary between rain and hot sun.

CONTACT:
Istanbul Marathon
Spor A.S, Genel Mudur/ugu
Karagumruk Mah, Kaleboyu Cad
No: 111 Fatih, Istanbul, Turkey
☎ +212 453 30 00
✉ info@istanbulmarathon.org
🖳 www.istanbulmarathon.org

WHILE YOU'RE THERE

This atmospheric city will always occupy your senses. When sightseeing, check opening hours; places have random opening times. The **Sultanahmet Topkapi Palace** is best visited early in the morning when there are fewer crowds. Be sure to check out the fourth courtyard and the (no longer operational) harem, which many miss. The **Blue Mosque** is worth a visit at night when there is always a sound and light show. By night the side streets around **Istiklal Street** boast lots of nightlife: chic café bars, bistros, restaurants, nightclubs, and music clubs such as Club 360. See: www.gototurkey.co.uk

The course then travels 4½ miles (7 km) along the west bank of the historic waterway before cutting across the only landward side of town to reach the Sea of Marmara.

From 12½–25 miles (20–40 km) runners go out and back to the west, returning around the seaward side of the 15th-century Topkapi Palace, home to the Ottoman Sultans, as the waterfront bends northward, turning into the Bosphorus. Over the final hilly half mile, runners take a left turn to run inland, ascending through the Palace Gardens and passing under the shadow of the Byzantine cathedral of Hagia Sophia to finish beside the 300-year-old Blue Mosque – so called because of the 20,000 blue tiles that cover its surface.

The race is in mid-October, and a 9:00 am start time almost guarantees comfortable running conditions. The going is fast, apart from the last half mile, as the course records of 2:10 and 2:27 would indicate. These were run very recently: the 1985 course record set by Turkey's own Mehmet Terzi took more than 20 years to break. Finally, in 2006, it was improved by a single second.

Istanbul possessed elevated status under the Byzantine Empire, with such grand titles as "The Great City" and "City of Emperors," and after taking part in such a prestigious race, runners will feel equally as grand. Those who come to run here say they have not just completed a physical challenge, but absorbed the atmosphere of one of the world's great cities.

Above: The Bosphorus Bridge is ¾ mile (1 km) long, and 100,000 competitors participate in the fun run and marathon.

Tallinn Marathon | Estonia

Estonia's ascendancy to the world marathon stage began in 1989, just two years before the country was declared independent from Russia. After many years of struggling to find numbers and favor with the city authorities, the marathon was recently relaunched after being canceled at extremely short notice in 2007. The new marathon has had an immediate impact, and a half marathon and 6-mile (10 km) run are now held at the same time.

In Berlin, London, and New York, you know what sights lie on the well-trodden marathon route. Head to Tallinn, the capital of Estonia, and you'll be continually surprised by what gems were hidden from view during the Cold War years. Tallinn provides runners with an abundance of history and culture. Locals are proud of their UNESCO World Heritage Site status, as well as their recent stint as the European Capital of Culture in 2011, something that has injected a spirit of optimism for the future of the Baltic. The city and the race are where folk culture meets blue-chip technology. The route begins in the new business district and moves to take in Tallinn's old quarters, embracing the parks, the old city walls, and an old town that is a renowned jewel. There is respite to be had in running along the coastal paths and beside beaches, to the east of the city leading to the Tallinn Marina and beyond.

In September runners can expect favorable running temperatures. Temperatures are usually cool, averaging 46–55°F (8–15°C). Such conditions have already secured Tallinn as the biggest marathon field in the Baltic, which, with those in the half marathon, 6-mile (10 km) run, and fun run added in, now totals more than 17,500. Just 1,000 among these run the marathon.

At the last count, 40 different nationalities were registered to run, which, given the previous low profile of the country, can be seen as instant success. Visitors have mostly come from Germany, Finland, Britain, and Russia, but more are flocking from landmark marathon countries as far as the US. Estonia has made it state policy to explore the advantages of wireless

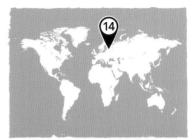

WHILE YOU'RE THERE

The medieval heart of Tallinn is called **Toompea** and is well worth a thorough exploration. What most people don't know is that Estonia has a stunning coastline, with beaches just 20 minutes away from the city center. Known as the Pirita District, it can seem a whole world away. **Pirita Beach** is 1¾ miles (3 km) of white sand, backed by windswept palms, and on a hot summer's day Estonians hit the resort en masse. See: www.tourism.tallinn.ee

communication, and the "green and keen" marathon organizers have followed this up with free rail travel to the race being texted to participants' mobile phones. Additionally, there is an enthusiasm to embrace the latest marathon technology.

Running here opens your eyes to a thriving community that is now relishing the opportunity to showcase itself. Just one weekend here will give you the chance to sample music shows, exhibitions, and some charming folk traditions – once you're out of your running shorts.

Left: A bird's-eye view of the start of the marathon.

Top: More than 10,000 runners throng the streets on marathon day, including children who have their own race.

Bottom: The Tallinn Marathon boasts some of the best value entry fees in Europe.

Right: Running the Tallinn Marathon is one of the best ways to see this undiscovered city from a fresh perspective.

RACE DETAILS

WHEN? September
WHEN TO APPLY: By April
HOW MANY TAKE PART? 12,500
DIFFICULTY RATING: 5/10
SPECIAL CONSIDERATIONS: As you reach the outer stretches of the city, support can be thin on the ground. Be aware, too, that the course covers some cobbled streets that can be hard on the ankles and knees.

CONTACT:
Talinn Marathon
MTÜ Spordiürituste Korraldamise Klubi
Sport Event Team
Pärnu mnt 142a
11317 Tallinn
Estonia
☎ 372 654 8462
✉ info@talinnmarathon.ee
🖥 www.tallinnmarathon.ee

Athens Classic Marathon | Greece

The road from Marathon to Athens is part of mythology. The Marathon legend started here in 490 BC, and it was resurrected here under the flag of the modern Olympic Games in 1896 to become synonymous with any act of sustained endeavor.

The legend has it that a soldier-messenger was sent from Marathon to Athens to announce the victory of the Greeks after they defeated a Persian army of far superior number. A more plausible, and more heroic, version of the story is that the Greek soldiers who had done battle at Marathon, all 11,000 of them, walk-ran from the site of the battle back to Athens to forestall a second landing by the Persian Army.

RACE DETAILS

WHEN? November
WHEN TO APPLY: January
HOW MANY TAKE PART? 12,000
DIFFICULTY RATING: 8/10
SPECIAL CONSIDERATIONS:
Considered one of the toughest marathons
in the world, largely due to the prevalence
of hills that continue for long stretches.
Temperatures can alternate quickly from
hot to cold, making it difficult to acclimate.

CONTACT:
Hellenic Athletics Federation (Segas)
137 Syngrou Avenue
171 21 Nea Smirini
Athens, Greece
☎ +30 210 933 1113/210 931 5886
✉ registrations@athensclassicmarathon.gr
🖥 www.athensclassicmarathon.gr

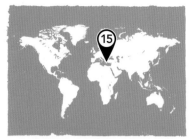

15

WHILE YOU'RE THERE

The Greek capital can be smoggy and claustrophobic, but its monuments, such as the **Parthenon,** are a must-see. Be sure to head out to the coast. For example, you can take an overnight ferry to Crete and visit the town of **Plakias,** where beaches are minutes away. Stay on the mainland and explore the Attican peninsula. Start off in Glyfada or Vouliagmeni and take the sea road to find the ruins of Sounion, the **Temple of Poseidon,** and the **Sanctuary of Athena.**

It is possible that the distance the soldiers ran was as much as 28 miles (45 km), but from the battle site to the centre of Athens it is around 25 miles (40 km), and this was the distance that was first established for the marathon in the inaugural modern Olympic Games held in Athens in 1896.

Following the 1908 Olympics in London, the marathon distance became standardized as 26.2 miles (42.2 km), and the extra 2,400 yards (2,195 m) has been added on in the Athens Classic Marathon as a respectful loop around the burial mound of the fallen Greek soldiers.

The original route was probably over steep terrain and would have been more like cross-country than road running. Today, there is a modern highway all the way from the marathon start point to the entrance to the stadium built for the 1896 Olympics. The tarmac may be smooth, but the road undulates upward from 6¾ miles (11 km) right through to the crest of the hills at 19¼ miles (31 km), before dropping down gently toward the center of Athens. To add yet more drama to the close of this historic race, the runners are overlooked by the Parthenon, gleaming white from the top of the nearby Acropolis.

You are likely to see many runners dressed up in the style of the ancient Greek military with helmets and costumes, but nothing can be as arduous as tackling the course while carrying real swords and full body armor, as the marathon pioneers may have done. In 2010 the race celebrated the 2,500th anniversary of the Battle of Marathon, and international interest was such that the 12,000 marathon places were snapped up in only three weeks.

The point-to-point route, from the site of the original battlefield in Marathon to the reconstructed stadium in Athens, means that runners are driven out in buses to the start, allowing them a last-minute preview of the route. Due to the event's momentous history, the course has been kept as close to the 1896 route as possible, but time has made it more agreeable to modern runners with proper road surfaces, hospitable crowds, and the benefits of comfortable running shoes.

Heading into Athens, there is an instant shift in noise, from the relative tranquility of the countryside to the traffic horns, buzz, and cheering crowds of the city. As supporters near the finishing line, children arrive armed with crowns made from olive-tree branches to place on the heads of soon-to-be heroes. As runners enter the final 109 yards (100 m) in the ancient white marble stadium (which was reconstructed from the remains of the ancient Greek stadium), they can mentally recreate their own imaginings of past glories. Those who take part in this event regard it as a privilege but will humbly tell you they consider their feat marginal when compared with the soldiers who first embarked on this journey through thick shrubbery and endured the pain of their battle scars. This is the event where competitors show their respect to those historic running legends.

Previous page: The finale to the marathon is in the spectacular white marble stadium, rebuilt from ancient ruins for the 1896 Olympic Games.

Above: The final 164 yards (150 m) is run in the marble Panathinaikos Stadium, which was the centerpiece of the first modern Olympic Games, and every step is infused with an emotion appropriate to the historic setting.

Midnight Sun Marathon | Norway

There are few places where running at night can be so exhilarating as at a latitude of 70 degrees north. The Midnight Sun Marathon is an arctic adventure for the running select, with 24 hours of daylight providing an almost unworldly experience.

The journey begins in Tromsø, 1,240 miles (2,000 km) from the North Pole. Although there is still snow on the hilltops that surround the town, it is a warm and welcoming place. Around 50,000 people live in Tromsø, the unofficial capital of northern Norway, a location that positively brims with culture. This land is defined by the natural majesty of the northern lights, polar nights, and midnight sun.

In summer, the sun doesn't set for two months. The distinctive atmosphere that this creates throughout the night provides a thrilling warm-up to the world's northernmost continental marathon. The climate is moderate enough, offering mild conditions on race day – summer weather ranges from 41–82°F (5–28°C). Runners from more than 60 nations take part, coming from the UK, USA, Germany, Sweden, Italy, Brazil, and Australia. Alongside the marathon, there is a half marathon, a 6-mile (10 km) race, and a mini-marathon, as well as a children's race.

The course begins with a loop into the city center before runners pass Fridtjof Nansen Square – named after the pioneering polar explorer – and climb up over the 3,360-foot (1,026 m) long Tromsø Bridge, which rises to 144 feet (44 m) above sea level. Reaching the mainland, runners pass the Arctic Cathedral and head down the coast road to a turning point after about 6 miles (10 km). Returning back over the bridge, the half marathoners peel off to the finish, but marathon runners go on through the center of the city and around the southern part of the island before heading north into the midnight sun. After another turnaround, the course returns to finish in the city center, where the town spills out onto the streets to cheer on the finishers with an uplifting fervor.

WHILE YOU'RE THERE

The locals celebrate hard at the end of a marathon. But be sure to reserve energy for some daytime exploration, as the region offers some of the most beautiful natural majesty in the world. This reveals itself in the **weather-beaten islands** of the Arctic Ocean, **blue fjords, glaciers,** and the towering peaks of the 5,900-foot (1,800 m) high **Lyngen Alps**. The tepid waters of the Gulf Stream ensure a mild climate at high latitude, offering maximum chance of experiencing the colorful rays of the **northern lights**, as well as the golden warmth of the midnight sun. See: www.visitnorway.com

The inhabitants of Tromsø regard the Midnight Sun Marathon as one of the big spectacles that brings the world to its doorstep. Other popular attractions in the city are the Arctic Cathedral, the Tromsø Museum, the Polar Museum, and a cable car that runs up a nearby hilltop. Despite its location in the far north of Norway, Tromsø has the cosmopolitan feel of a larger city, with inhabitants from 130 different countries, a vibrant nightlife, and charming coffee shops, bars, and restaurants. Just a short distance outside the city lies one of Norway's most photogenic regions with fjords and mountains aplenty, crowned by snow even in midsummer.

Below: The Midnight Sun Marathon begins at 8:30 pm in the evening and has enthusiastic crowd support.

RACE DETAILS

WHEN? June
WHEN TO APPLY: December of the year before
HOW MANY TAKE PART? 1,000
DIFFICULTY RATING: 7/10
SPECIAL CONSIDERATIONS: You are up close to nature. It is not uncommon to see wild animals such as bears en route. Flights and accommodations are booked up quickly, so start arranging these details as early as possible.

CONTACT:
Midnight Sun Marathon
PB821, N-9258 Tromsø
☎ +47 77 67 33 63
✉ post@msm.no
🖥 www.msm.no

RACE DETAILS

WHEN? October
WHEN TO APPLY: April to August
HOW MANY TAKE PART? 4,000
DIFFICULTY RATING: 5/10
SPECIAL CONSIDERATIONS: The race goes across long stretches of the Danube, which can be monotonous, and support can be sparse when compared with bigger events. Give yourself plenty of time to reach the start on race day.

CONTACT:
Budapest Marathon Organisation
H-1138 Budapest,
Váci út 152-156.
Hungary
☎ +36 1 273 0939
✉ budapest.run@futanet.hu
🖥 www.budapestmarathon.com

Budapest Marathon | Hungary

Hungary's capital offers a culture-rich experience for the runner and the traveler alike. It is a city of architectural splendor that spreads along the broad sweep of the Danube River, and its marathon takes you on a tour through the very best parts.

Budapest was once two separate cities, but the town of Buda, nestling among the hills of the Danube's west bank, was united with Pest, on the flat eastern bank, in 1873.

For much of its length, the course runs along the lower embankments of the river, affording a panorama of the Buda Hills from the Pest side and views of the magnificent Neo-Gothic dome Parliament House from the Buda side, as well as crossing two, and sometimes three, of the famous Danube bridges.

The race starts in the iconic statue-lined Hosök Tere, or Heroes' Square, and loops back to finish nearby after its grand tour of the Hungarian capital. The heroes referred to are not of the Soviet era (although a giant statue of Stalin that was once sited close to the present finish line was toppled from its plinth in the 1956 Hungarian Uprising). Heroes' Square was built in 1896 to mark the millennium of the founding of the Hungarian state, and the statuary lining the monument's porticoes are primarily those of previous kings. Runners exit the impressive open square along the tree-lined Andrássy út, a UNESCO World Heritage Site, passing Béla Bartók Memorial Museum and the majestic Hungarian State Opera House. It joins the Pest embankment before making a northward loop as far as a turning point opposite Margaret Island. It then returns to cross the Danube to Buda by means of the iconic Chain Bridge, the first permanent link between the two sides of the river, originally built in 1849.

Runners join the embankment under the ramparts of Buda Castle and turn north to the second turning point – beyond the first, but on the opposite side of the river. Retracing their steps south, runners reach the third turning point after passing under the Chain Bridge and beyond the Rudas Thermal Bath, the Art Deco Gellért Hotel, and the Technical University.

Left: Looking south down Andrássy út as runners leave Heroes' Square at the start of the race.

Runners then cross back over the Danube by means of Liberty Bridge and run about 3 miles (5 km) northward on the Buda embankment. Finally, turning away from the river in front of the Parliament, the last mile or so confronts you with the biggest rise on this almost entirely flat course – a flyover taking runners over the inner ring road, a route necessary to avoid closing Europe's busiest tram system.

Like the other capital of the Habsburg "dual-monarchy" Empire, Vienna, Budapest makes music a theme of the marathon, with classical concerts performing in full swing as the race comes to an end. Tired runners can flock to Budapest's many spas, which are a welcome delight to ease the pains of the runners. Choose

Left: The Chain Bridge is the first that runners cross in the Budapest Marathon.

Above: Much of the on-course support has to come from fellow runners still approaching the turns after you have made yours, as the lower embankments leave little room for bystanders.

the 19th-century Szechenyi Bath and Spa conveniently close to the finish line in the City Park, or return to the Rudas Thermal Baths in Buda, dating from the 16th and 17th centuries and redolent with atmosphere. The evocative surroundings and the promise of a thermal bath at the end of the race make the Budapest Marathon an inviting prospect.

Cape Town Marathon and Two Oceans Marathon | South Africa

Table Mountain in Cape Town provides a stunningly beautiful backdrop, and there are several races organized to take advantage of it. The Cape Town Marathon is run in September, and the more high-profile Two Oceans Marathon – which is a 35-mile (56 km) ultra-distance race – is held on Easter Saturday each year, along with a highly popular half marathon.

Like races all over South Africa, the Cape Town Marathon starts at 6:30 am to take advantage of the cooler conditions. Water stations are placed regularly throughout the course to ensure that runners stay well hydrated. The fast, flat route of the marathon starts in Cape Town's city center and takes runners out to Rondebosch before looping back to the city and the Victoria & Alfred Waterfront, Sea Point, and the Green Point Common.

Many runners turn out for the Cape Town Marathon to chase times that will qualify them to run in one of South Africa's racing spectacles, such as the Comrades Marathon in Durban (55 miles/ 89 km), or more locally, the Two Oceans Marathon.

WHILE YOU'RE THERE

The **Victoria & Alfred Waterfront** offers the sight of one of the most beautiful natural harbors in the world. Take advantage of the hotels – the **Table Bay Hotel** offers great views across the ocean to **Robben Island** and the best afternoon teas in the country, with many traveling from afar to sample the delicacies on offer (www.hoteltablebay.co.za). Nearby is the **Cape Grace**, best visited in the evening for Africa's finest collection of whisky.

Left: A flat, fast course amid spectacular scenery of mountains and sea make this an appealing marathon.

Right: The Two Oceans Marathon and its associated trail run (pictured) lives up to its reputation as a tough endurance run.

RACE DETAILS

CAPE TOWN MARATHON
WHEN? September
WHEN TO APPLY: By June
HOW MANY TAKE PART? 1,800
DIFFICULTY RATING: 7/10
SPECIAL CONSIDERATIONS: Early start and lonely roads, as well as sweat-inducing heat, so keep an eye on hydration.

CONTACT:
PO Box 101
Lansdowne
7779 Cape Town, South Africa

☎ +27 21 699 0655
🖳 www.wpa.org.za

TWO OCEANS MARATHON 56KM
WHEN? Easter Saturday
WHEN TO APPLY: October
HOW MANY TAKE PART? 11,000
(16,000 in half marathon)
DIFFICULTY RATING: 8/10
SPECIAL CONSIDERATIONS: It is an ultra-marathon of 35 miles (56 km), not a standard marathon, so extra training is a must. Plenty of hills, inclines and challenges, the 7-hour cutoff time leaves many disappointed. Heat can take its toll.

CONTACT:
Old Mutual Two Oceans Marathon
PO Box 2276
Clareinch 7740
Cape Town
South Africa
☎ +27 21 657 5140
✉ info@twooceansmarathon.org.za
🖳 www.twooceansmarathon.org.za

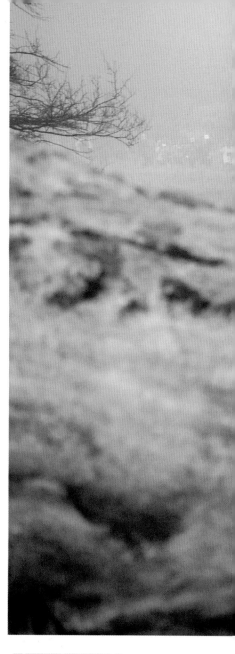

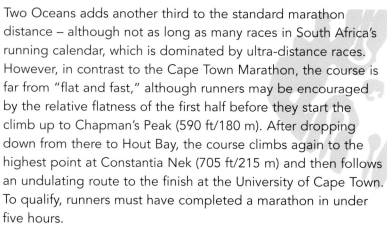

Two Oceans adds another third to the standard marathon distance – although not as long as many races in South Africa's running calendar, which is dominated by ultra-distance races. However, in contrast to the Cape Town Marathon, the course is far from "flat and fast," although runners may be encouraged by the relative flatness of the first half before they start the climb up to Chapman's Peak (590 ft/180 m). After dropping down from there to Hout Bay, the course climbs again to the highest point at Constantia Nek (705 ft/215 m) and then follows an undulating route to the finish at the University of Cape Town. To qualify, runners must have completed a marathon in under five hours.

Left: There is much truth in the organizers' claim that the Two Ocean Marathon is "the world's most beautiful marathon" despite the fact that it is not technically a marathon.

Above: Wild, windy weather can make conditions difficult for even the most experienced runners.

The Two Oceans route takes in the gardens of Kirstenbosch and the vast sweep of coastline from Fish Hoek, cutting through the Cape Town peninsula to Chapman's Peak. In doing so, it lives up to its name and takes in the coastlines of the Atlantic and Indian Oceans in one glorious sweep.

The tipping point comes during the mountain climb known as the "Suikerbossie Pass." When all reserves are spent, the reward is the sight of the Atlantic Ocean glistening in the distance, and the memory of it will stay with you for years.

RACE DETAILS

WHEN? End of May/start of June
WHEN TO APPLY: January of the same year
HOW MANY TAKE PART? 21,000
DIFFICULTY RATING: 7/10
SPECIAL CONSIDERATIONS: Unlike many marathons, this one starts in the afternoon, so if the weather is scorching, conditions can become uncomfortable.

CONTACT:
Stockholm Marathon
15124, SE-16715 Bromma
Sweden
☎ +46 8 545 664 40
✉ info@marathon.se
🖥 www.stockholmmarathon.se

Stockholm Marathon
Sweden

The story of Stockholm's marathon shows that with grit and determination, almost anyone can complete a marathon. Anders Olsson founded the Stockholm Marathon to boost the profile of distance running in Scandinavia. He remembers, "On my long journey home on the subway one November day in 1978, I was dazzled by an article in *Sports Illustrated* magazine. It was about the New York City Marathon, with 21,000 runners pacing the streets across the Big Apple. I was really inspired. What a contrast to the lukewarm and isolated Swedish running scene. This was a race to attend. But then I had second thoughts. Why should you have to go to New York? Couldn't we replicate the success story in Stockholm?"

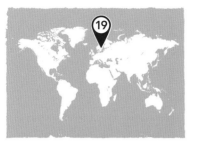

WHILE YOU'RE THERE

Sweden's capital is home to a vast, fan-shaped maritime world of more than 24,000 islets. In summer, the **Archipelago** is a paradise for sailors and boaters and also accessible to visitors traveling by public transit. An hour by bus, local train, or car will take you to various island communities.

The best option, however, is to depart from central Stockholm on one of the **classic white ferries**, many of which date from the 19th and early 20th centuries. Once there, you can explore the sheer natural beauty of the islands – most are well served with **hotels**, **inns**, **campsites**, and **restaurants**.
See: www.visitsweden.com

Inspired by this vision, Olsson had to persuade other athletics enthusiasts that it was an achievable idea and, more of a challenge, ask the police authorities to close off the roads. Back in the 1970s, marathon running was something out of the ordinary, the reserve of eccentrics. "Generally they ran on dusty country roads with no spectators apart from some loyal wives and a few amused bystanders," Olsson recounted. By August 1979, the Stockholm Marathon was ready to launch, with more than 2,000 entries. That was just the start. The streets were packed with spectators, the roads closed off, and an enthusiastic public gathered in anticipation, not knowing quite what to expect.

The course is run over two laps, which makes it all the more crowded, as many spirited spectators line the route. The route is varied, winding its way through woods, past water, and then taking in the historic sites of the Swedish capital. The marathon climaxes in the 1912 Olympic Stadium, with thousands of fans

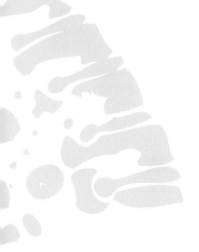

Previous page: Runners pass along the waterside around the old town in Stockholm.

Left: The course takes in two laps around the medieval city, the waterways, and forest.

Above: The run begins outside the 1912 Olympic Stadium and finishes on a track inside, to much enthusiastic crowd support.

waiting to cheer on those who have finished. The stadium has been the venue for 83 world records, and with 8,500 international runners from more than 81 countries, this marathon is a multicultural festival.

Part of the draw is Stockholm, one of the world's most beautiful capitals. Built on 14 islands around its medieval city center, it is superbly positioned, with stunning scenic views in every direction. The archipelago of 24,000 islets is waiting to be explored just outside the city. Stockholm is a city of contrasts – water and islands, history and innovation, small town and big city, long summer nights and short winter days. The course embraces the best of the capital, heading into the woods of the Royal Djurgården Park and through the streets of the city center, passing buildings such as the Royal Palace, the City Hall, the Royal Opera, and the Houses of Parliament. Crossing the high, arching Västerbron Bridge at the western end of the course, runners are rewarded with a fantastic view of the city.

Vienna City Marathon | Austria

The race slogan of the Vienna City Marathon is "Run Vienna, Enjoy Classics," and this spirit is borne out in a number of ways, from runners in Amadeus wigs to mini classical concerts along the route. This is a race run against a backdrop of classical Hapsburg architecture and an accompaniment of classical music from great composers – after all, this was Mozart's city.

Vienna has inspired musicians with its rich classical past. Its effect on runners is little different. The unexpected melody of a string quartet will lift the spirit when their energy levels flag. To onlookers, it is a race set to an operatic soundtrack. In fact, you may often be buoyed along the route by the music of composers such as Mozart and Strauss. In previous years the much-revered Sir Simon Rattle has conducted special concerts for the race.

Runners come from more than 100 countries to make up a total field of 30,000. The course includes many long, flat stretches of road and expanses of greenery. The scenic tour of the city is enough to keep morale up. This is a good venue for first-timers.

WHILE YOU'RE THERE

Be sure to head to the **Hofburg Castle**, once the heart of the Austro-Hungarian Empire and now the heart of Vienna – its parks, churches, and museums all surround it. Meander through the lanes and the world-famous coffee houses, the rendez-vous of many an intellectual.
If you want to go further astray, head to **Belvedere Palace** in the 3rd District, the hub of Vienna's classical art collection, including Gustav Klimt's *The Kiss*. Equally impressive is the **Schönbrunn Palace**. It was built to rival France's Versailles in Baroque beauty, but the House of Habsburg lacked the funds to outdo its French rival. See: www.austria.info

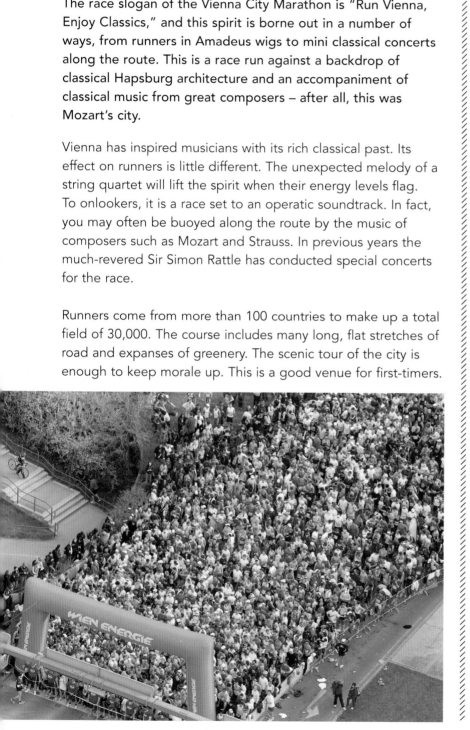

Left: Other runs take place at the same time as the marathon in this attractive and scenic city.

Right: The Vienna City Marathon attracts many elite athletes.

RACE DETAILS

WHEN? April
WHEN TO APPLY: By November of the year before
HOW MANY TAKE PART? 30,000
DIFFICULTY RATING: 5/10
SPECIAL CONSIDERATIONS: Cutoff time here is 6 hours, but the clearing up operation can happen before that.

CONTACT:
Enterprise Sport Promotion GmbH
Gußhausstruße 21/19
1040 Vienna, Austria
☎ +43 1 606 421 95 10
✉ office@vienna-marathon.com
🖳 www.vienna-marathon.com

In fact, one edition of the race limited the elite field to "debutantes only."

The race begins with a long, straight crossing of the Donaukanal (Danube canal), passing beside the city's UN Building, and finishes by turning off the inner ring road under an archway. Abruptly you find yourself at the Heldenplatz (or Heroes' Square), right in front of the Imperial Palace. Along the route you cross the Danube, past the iconic Ferris Wheel in Wiener Prater (Prater Park), and run in front of the Schönbrunn Palace. The Opera House is perhaps the classical building that has made the city so recognizable around the world, and it is also included in the runners' tour offered by the marathon.

Above: Athletes from more than 100 countries take part in this popular event.

Right: The Vienna City Marathon was among the first to offer technical assistance to its runners and their supporters. It pioneered a text messaging service that alerted participants to split times recorded every 3 miles (5 km), allowing any runner's progress to be tracked and their finishing time anticipated.

The crowds are vocal, and their support is always welcome. Even as a stranger you will still feel as if your own relatives are urging you on toward the finishing line. The support is not just confined to the race. Race organizers have created a network to encourage runners to come to Vienna from afar. The VCM Friendship Runners are local volunteers who have run the race before and can assist newcomers by answering questions and exchanging information in their own language, through the website: www.vienna-marathon.com.

The handling of this event is superbly organized and not without elements of fun. Each year the marathon is themed around a key event. In 2010 this included celebrating the 2,500-year anniversary of the Battle of Marathon in Greece.

Prague Marathon | Czech Republic

The Prague Marathon has become a bold and cosmopolitan symbol of the Czech Republic's approach to life and its management of the city.

Many claimed it would be impossible to organize a marathon through the cobbled streets of Prague, but race founder Carlo Capalbo thought otherwise. He enlisted the support of the Czech sporting legend Emil Zátopek, who won three gold medals at the Helsinki Olympics in 1952, and the 1988 Italian Olympic Marathon Champion Gelindo Bordin. Together they set about organizing an international marathon in this city of ancient lanes, stunning architecture, and an often tumultuous history.

RACE DETAILS

WHEN? May
WHEN TO APPLY: By January
HOW MANY TAKE PART? 11,000
DIFFICULTY RATING: 6/10
SPECIAL CONSIDERATIONS: Recent participants have reported logistical problems at the start, and the narrow cobblestone streets can be difficult for those with ankle or knee problems.

CONTACT:
Prague Marathon
Záhoranského 3
120 00 Prague 2
Czech Republic
☎ +420 224 91 92 09
✉ info@praguemarathon.com
🖥 www.praguemarathon.com

(21)

WHILE YOU'RE THERE

Prague is one of the most well-preserved cities in Europe, and a meander through the **old city** reveals fascinating sites. An essential is a visit to the **Charles Bridge**, which is as much a work of art as it is a feat of engineering. Spend an afternoon wandering across and up to the medieval **Prague Castle**, marveling at the architecture, including Gothic, Renaissance, and Art Nouveau.

Since its foundation in 1995, when just 958 runners lined up at the start of the race, the Prague Marathon has grown into one of the most magical and exciting international marathons.

Prague is a city that is animated by the arts. The Marathon Music Festival is held alongside the race and hosts professional and amateur bands all along the course, setting the beat for runners' steps. The music attracts crowds onto the streets, providing support for the runners and creating an inviting atmosphere. The Prague race begins each year with a rendition of the beloved Czech theme "Vltava," from Bedrich Smetana's composition "Ma Vlast" (My Country), a piece of music that is reminiscent of the sound of a flowing river. As the music plays, the composition seems to embrace the river of runners flooding over the start line at the Old Town Square. From the starting gun, they begin their swift flow through the streets and alongside the Vltava River.

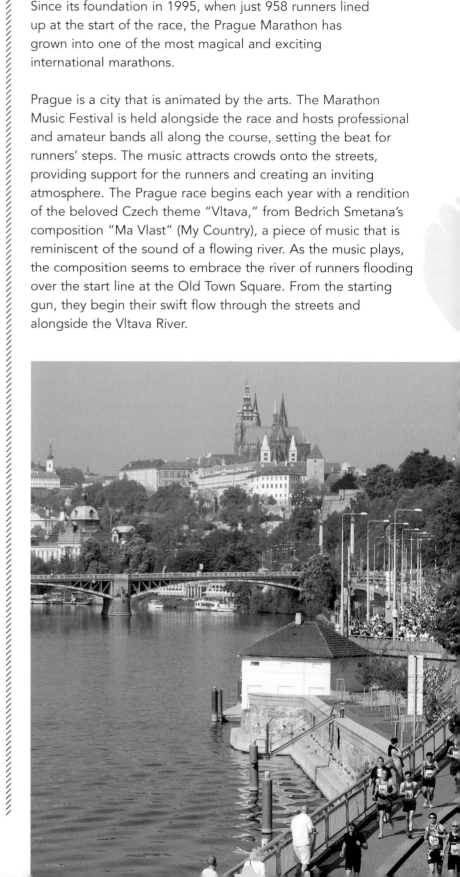

Reaching the river after about a thousand feet (a few hundred meters), runners benefit from views of Prague Castle – the ancient seat of Czech kings and the current seat of the Czech President – on the other side. Runners pass the Czech Parliament, the Rudolfinum Concert Hall, and the Municipal Hall, where every year, following the marathon, the Prague Spring Music Festival begins. Still only in about the first 1¼ miles (the second kilometer), the course then passes through the National Library Quarter, National Theater, and Prague Karolinum, the seat of Charles University, the oldest university in Central Europe.

The course then crosses back over the river by the famous Charles Bridge, which forms the logo of the Prague Marathon. Treading in the footsteps of more recent history, runners pass down the National Avenue, where the former Czechoslovakia's post-communist era began in the student-led Velvet Revolution on 17 November 1989. The final 440 yards (400 m) follows the first part of the course in reverse.

Below: The Prague waterfront is an attractive route for runners.

Below right: The old city monuments are never far away in this marathon.

Bottom right: Paris (Parizska) street is Prague's most famous shopping street, which is always packed with thousands of spectators cheering the runners on to the finishing line.

Berlin Marathon | Germany

The BMW Berlin Marathon is a race where German reserve is broken and emotions run high. It is known as the course where the most world records have been set and where tears are often shed at the Brandenburg Gate finishing line.

Every aspect of the environment is conducive to running. There is the flat and even course, the mild autumn weather, and the atmosphere of the crowd that ripples like an electric current to spur even the most exhausted runners home. Competition is high for amateurs and elite participants alike – elite runners petition for a place in Berlin because they know the course is so favorable for fast times (Paula Radcliffe came here to achieve an Olympic qualifying time in 2011).

More than 40,000 participants take part in the race, and spectators flock to the streets, alongside more than 70 live bands. In some spots, the race becomes a carnival – especially at "Wilde Eber," around 16¾ miles (27 km) into the race, where a group of cheerleaders raise the tempo as the course crests and then gently descends toward the Kurfürstendamm.

The first Berlin Marathon was staged in the Grunewald forest in 1974 in the southwest of the city. It came out of the woods and onto the streets of West Berlin in 1981, but it was only in 1990, after the fall of the Berlin Wall, that the marathon burst through the Brandenburg Gate and embraced the old East Berlin. This was a landmark marathon event that ranks alongside the great centennial 1996 Boston Marathon, or the cathartic 2001 New York City race, just weeks following the 9/11 attacks.

The course now weaves its way past Berlin's historic landmarks, such as the Reichstag, Potsdamer Platz, and Berliner Dom, and climaxes at the Brandenburg Gate just 383 yards (350 m) before the finish line. Berlin's architecture provides an animated tour of its history, and running a marathon through it is the best possible way to experience the sights in a few hours.

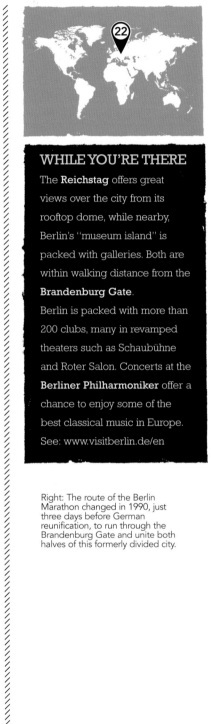

WHILE YOU'RE THERE

The **Reichstag** offers great views over the city from its rooftop dome, while nearby, Berlin's "museum island" is packed with galleries. Both are within walking distance from the **Brandenburg Gate**.
Berlin is packed with more than 200 clubs, many in revamped theaters such as Schaubühne and Roter Salon. Concerts at the **Berliner Philharmoniker** offer a chance to enjoy some of the best classical music in Europe. See: www.visitberlin.de/en

Right: The route of the Berlin Marathon changed in 1990, just three days before German reunification, to run through the Brandenburg Gate and unite both halves of this formerly divided city.

RACE DETAILS

WHEN? Last weekend of September
WHEN TO APPLY: By January
HOW MANY TAKE PART? 40,000
DIFFICULTY RATING: 4/10
SPECIAL CONSIDERATIONS: Due to the volume of runners, the course can become overcrowded at some points. Fast and flat course.

CONTACT:
BMW Berlin Marathon
SCC Events GmbH
Hanns-Brau-Strasse
Adlerplatz
14053 Berlin, Germany
☎ +49 30 30 12 88 10
✉ info@sccevents.com
🖳 www.bmwberlin-marathon.com

RACE DETAILS

WHEN? May
WHEN TO APPLY: December of the year before
HOW MANY TAKE PART? 12,000
DIFFICULTY RATING: 5/10
SPECIAL CONSIDERATIONS: Congestion at the finishing line means there is little space to meet up with supporters. Cobblestones on the route might make it tricky if you have ankle problems.

CONTACT:
Copenhagen Marathon
Gunnar Nu Hansens Plads 11
DK 2100, Copenhagen, Denmark
☎ +45 35 26 69 00
✉ info@copenhagenmarathon.dk
🖥 www.copenhagenmarathon.dk

Den Kongelige
Afstøbningssamling

MUSEUM
for KUNST

Copenhagen Marathon | Denmark

Some races are about the scenery and some are about the spirit of the event, but Copenhagen is all about the running. Competition is keen, and even the most amateur enthusiasts are rivals.

This dedication to running is defined in the unofficial slogan of the Copenhagen Marathon "It's all about the race." Even so, you'll still be taken on a tour around the iconic landmarks of the Danish capital. There is the Little Mermaid statue down by the harbor, the grand Parliament Building, and all around is the fresh, reviving air of the lakes, parks, and green spaces. The run takes in all facets of this city, from family-friendly districts to the finishing line at Langebro, with views over the waterfront. Runners are well serviced en route, with hydration stations every 2¾ miles (4.5 km) offering energy drinks, toilets, showers, and tubs of petroleum jelly to relieve the inevitable chafing sores.

Copenhagen welcomes new runners and has set up pace-setting groups to assist first-timers. A leading athletics group, the Sparta Club, groups runners according to their expected finishing time, helping them to ease through the course at a rhythm that will allow them to reach the finish within their target time. The slowest groups finish in 5 hours, making room for walking breaks, toilet stops, and throwing in heavy doses of morale-boosting songs and inspiration. If you find yourself flagging in one group, you can find another slower group, all clearly identifiable by pace runners carrying balloons.

Copenhagen's tradition of communal space allows runners coming here to feel part of one big family. Much of the route is through family districts, where spectators enjoy bacon sandwiches in between rousing cheers. There is a mini-marathon of ¾ mile (1 km) for children as part of the race's Sports Expo. The Expo is a meeting place full of energy and pre-race adrenaline, where you can buy running gear or get a warm-up massage.

Left: In Copenhagen every detail has been addressed, so you can concentrate on the one big reason for coming – the race.

WHILE YOU'RE THERE

Copenhagen has an excellent public transport system, including its world-famous city bikes used by visitors and locals alike. The city of Copenhagen keeps expanding its network of **bicycle lanes** and routes, and you are likely to get around town faster by bike than by any other means.

The **harbor cruise** is a great introduction to the beauty of the **medieval city**, including the **17th-century stock exchange** and **Nybrogade**.

Venice Marathon | Italy

The question for the Venice Marathon organization team was how to stage a marathon within a place famous for the lack of any significant land. The answer was to utilize the many bridges that span the floating city of Venice. Bridges are so crucial to this race that one is specially created for the event, a 557-foot (170 m) floating construction that straddles the Grand Canal. The pontoon gives runners a 360-degree view of central Venice and its most famous square, St. Mark's. Such views are not available to anyone but the marathon runners; not even the well-heeled tourists who pay five-figure sums for lavish hotel suites can secure a fine view. The prominence of the bridges is highlighted by the fact that during the final 1¾ miles (3 km) of the marathon, there are 13 bridges to cross.

The start of the marathon is on the mainland in front of the 18th-century Villa Pisani, in a village called Stra that was originally built for Italian nobility. The route heads through the countryside toward the industrial town of Mestre, reached after 15½ miles (25 km). This is a part of the course that you may never see in the photographs. Beyond lies the large green space of San Giuliano Park, in which runners complete a 1¼-mile (2 km) section and ready themselves for the 3-mile (5 km) crossing of Ponta della Liberta, or Liberty Bridge, the causeway leading to Venice itself. It is here that the frontrunners make their bid to win, but those setting their own pace may find that appreciating the view of the Venetian skyline, looming ever closer, slows their progress a little. Once you're in the town, the view changes to a series of more urban close-ups, apart from the amazing views of supporters from the pontoon bridge.

Negotiating the bridges demands care and attention. Past the finish line, the water becomes something to be sought out rather than avoided as runners soak their tired legs in the lagoon and find food, drink, massages, and a change of clothes arriving by water taxi. But running through Venice at marathon-time helps you get a glimpse of a city that is unknown to other visitors, sweeping in and out of tight alleyways, canal-side paths, and gaping squares. The event's officially adopted charity, Water Aid, fits in neatly with its exhortation to "Run for Water, Run for Life."

WHILE YOU'RE THERE

Venetians love their football, as you would expect of any Italian city. Here, if you wish to spectate, you arrive at the stadium in the historic center by water. After the match there is a great pub crawl along **Via Garibaldi**, where drink prices beat the average tourist traps. Alternatively, grab a seat in one of the local pubs screening Italian Serie A matches. **The Rialto Market,** with its noisy fishmongers and colorful vegetable stalls, is surrounded by many bars, and this is where most of Venice converges for weekend feasts.

Right: If you want to take part, make sure you book early – entries are limited to 6,000 each year to prevent undue wear and tear on this World Heritage Site.

RACE DETAILS

WHEN? October
WHEN TO APPLY: January to March
HOW MANY TAKE PART? 6,000
DIFFICULTY RATING: 5/10
SPECIAL CONSIDERATIONS: Lots of narrow stretches and many bridges to cross. Numbers are capped at 6,000, so early applications are necessary. Book accommodation far in advance.

CONTACT:
Venice Marathon Club
via Linghindal,
5/5-30172 Venezia Mestre
Italy

☎ +39 41 532 18 71
🖳 www.venicemarathon.it

Rome Marathon | Italy

For the experience of "running through history,"
no other marathon is quite like Rome because
it takes in an amazing number of historical landmarks.
The Colosseum, Vatican City, and the Trevi Fountain
are just a few of the delights on offer. These scenic
benefits are explained because Rome is saturated with
ancient and dramatic landmarks, but also because the
center of the city is closed off for marathon day, giving
runners the best that the city can offer.

RACE DETAILS

WHEN? March
WHEN TO APPLY: October of the year before
HOW MANY TAKE PART? 16,000
DIFFICULTY RATING: 6/10
SPECIAL CONSIDERATIONS: Highly praised for its scenery, but the frequency of cobbled streets might pose problems for some. Bring your own energy gels. Can get congested and hot in places.

CONTACT:
Viale B, Maratona di Roma
Bardanzellu 65,
00155 Roma
Italy

☎ +39 06 40 65064
🖥 www.maratonadiroma.it

Art, beauty, history, and the Italian way of life are all to be found in Rome. There are 500 landmarks along the course, including St. Paul's Basilica, the Villa Borghese, the Circus Maximus, and the Spanish Steps. **The Colosseum** is everyone's must-see while in Rome, but beware of hawkers dressed in Roman outfits, who'll charge a fortune for a photo. Be wary of tourist traps, for example, in **espresso bars;** always stand up to sip your coffee – cafés can charge four times as much if they serve you at a table.

The race starts and finishes in the shadow of Rome's most imposing of monuments, the Colosseum. Two millennia ago it might have been filled to its capacity of 50,000 people, when a significant gladiator fight was promised. Today, every year on the third Sunday in March, there are still 50,000 frenzied humans cheering with excitement – but they are outside on the road, awaiting the start of the marathon. There are 14,000 participants, and another 80,000 take part in the 2½-mile (4 km) "RomaFun" run that follows on the marathon runners' heels a few minutes later.

The serpentine course snakes its way south past the gigantic Circus Maximus, the Roman venue for chariot racing, to St. Paul's Basilica, then returns to the center along the banks of the Tiber. Then it strikes west across the river to St. Peter's Basilica and Vatican City. From here it goes north to the Foro Italico before looping back, again along the river, to the historical center. A final

Previous page: Runners pass through the Piazza del Popolo.

Above: Cobbled streets add to the charm of the old city, but wear cushioned running shoes to avoid very sore legs and feet.

Top right: The Rome Marathon is a perfect tourist marathon, taking in all the ancient sites.

Bottom right: Reviews have only positive things to say about this well-supported marathon.

flourish, almost like a premature lap of honor, takes runners on a tour of the Piazza del Popolo, the Villa Borghese, the Spanish Steps, and the Trevi Fountain. Marathons in other European capitals offer a sprinkling of sights separated by long suburban or commercial stretches, but every step run through the Eternal City brings another twist, another vista, and another marvel.

The weather is generally mild and the course is surprisingly flat, managing to avoid all seven of the hills on which the city is famously built. Fast times have been recorded here, indicating that the cobbled streets around the Colosseum at the start and finish – 1¼ miles (2 km) of them to start and 2½ miles (4 km) of them to finish – are no impediment.

For marathon runners more than others, all roads lead to Rome. It is fitting to recall that Rome has been the scene of epic sporting events for more than 3,000 years, and the drama of the modern marathon lives up to this legacy.

RACE DETAILS

WHEN? April
WHEN TO APPLY: August of the year before
HOW MANY TAKE PART? 15,000
DIFFICULTY RATING: 5/10
SPECIAL CONSIDERATIONS: Some narrow stretches of track might make this course seem claustrophobic at times. Easy to access from subways and bus stations.

CONTACT:
Marathon Hamburg Veranstaltungs GmbH
Alsterdorfer Strasse 262
22297 Hamburg
Germany
☎ +49 1805 77 17 60
✉ office@hamburgmarathon.de
🖥 www.marathon-hamburg.de

Hamburg Marathon | Germany

This is the city where The Beatles were introduced to the world, and its marathon is just as keen to swing to a different rhythm. Here you'll be swept along with the pounding footsteps of 15,000 marathon runners and the best crowd support of any long-distance race. Cries of "du schaffst es" (you can do it!) keep runners resolved to the finish.

It is the huge crowds that rally the marathon spirit, with enthusiastic supporters blowing whistles, horns, and trumpets, or bashing out tempo on pots and pans from their homes overlooking the course. There are an estimated 25 supporters for every one runner, so the race turns into a 26-mile (42 km) party. Perhaps the most heartening feature is that the support is at its loudest at the 18-mile (30 km) point, when many runners need it most.

The first thing that hits you about the Hamburg Marathon is how easy it is to get to. Subway stations stop right beside the starting point. Hamburg ensures all participants are well looked after, with water available every 1½ miles (2.5 km) and energy drinks every 3 miles (5 km). There are plenty of tubs of water along the course for dipping hats, sponges, or anything you want to cool down with.

The course here is flat but tightly packed with runners. Hamburg has been described as Germany's most livable city, and you feel something of this in the spirit that flows along the course come marathon day. At the pre-race Expo, newcomers can take a bus tour around the course, so they can become acquainted with it before the events begin.

Hamburg is one of the biggest ports in Europe, with a photogenic city combining docklands, canals, classic market squares, churches, and vast lakes. All of these are taken in during the race, as well as the suburbs that most visitors don't have a chance to see. The bridges and alleyways that create the atmosphere of this harbo-r town are all included.

Left: It is customary to finish off proceedings with steines of beer, a sauna, or fresh fish from the city's famous seafood market.

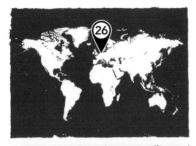

WHILE YOU'RE THERE

The city is known as the "green city of the Elbe" as more than half of the metropolitan area is covered in **green space and parks**. In fact, there are reputed to be more trees than people in this city.

By far the most spectacular recent addition to the city landscape is the **Hamburg Opera House**, opened in 2012 and second only in prominence to Sydney's famous landmark. It has been more than 325 years since culture-loving Germans had their own opera house in Hamburg. The **Reeperbahn** is great for a night out and for retracing the steps of The Beatles. See: www.hamburg-tourism.de/en

Frankfurt Marathon | Germany

A century ago indoor marathons were an established format – an alternative to the country lanes on which the first marathons were run. During the 1908 London Olympics, the Italian Dorando Pietri was "assisted" across the finish line and then disqualified amid great furor in favor of the American Johnny Hayes. Because of the massive public interest in this drama, a number of indoor marathons were staged around this time as spectacles for enthusiastic crowds who paid high entry fees.

Today, marathons are all about taking over city streets, a stretch of desert, or a Caribbean island to create a dramatic and exhilarating course for runners and spectators alike, but the Frankfurt Marathon harks back to the spirit of these early marathons. The final 109 yards (100 m) of this city-stomping extravaganza takes runners inside the city's Festival Hall.

Once inside, you'll realize that the venue's name is an appropriate one. As the runners pour in, they are greeted by fireworks, brass bands, and 10,000 spectators. Call it an Oktoberfest high on running, rather than total inebriation. This detail alone makes the race special, turning the atmosphere into something more like a concert than an outdoor marathon.

If the finish is a novelty, so too is the starting lineup. In the past this has been used as a setting to stage a make-believe murder – a drama acted out for the benefit of the television cameras. The plot sees a detective targeted by an escaped prisoner whom he had helped to incarcerate. Before the race, the prisoner attempts to shoot the private eye, only to hit an innocent fun runner instead. The rest of the drama ensues, with the prisoner giving chase through the race to catch his victim.

Frankfurt is a business city, with chrome-finished buildings that town planners commissioned to follow the style of the skyline of Manhattan or Chicago. Squint your eyes and you'll see there is a similarity.

WHILE YOU'RE THERE

There is a labyrinth of historical and modern buildings renowned for their artistic wonder. Highlights include the **Städel Institute of Art**, housing paintings from the Middle Ages, and the **Liebighaus**, boasting fine displays of sculpture. Waiting on the other side of the river is the **Museum of Modern Art** and the **Schirn Gallery**. There are a total of 60 museums in Frankfurt, all of which hold internationally acclaimed collections.

Right: The indoor finish along a red carpet provides an unusual finale to the Frankfurt Marathon.

The Frankfurt Marathon attracts about 21,000 participants and 35,000 spectators along the entire route, with around 9,500 running the full distance every year. The course runs in the shadow of the skyscrapers and takes in other landmarks, such as the Italian Renaissance-style Alte Oper – one of Europe's finest opera houses up until its destruction in 1944, and then, once again, when it was rebuilt and restored to its former glory in 1981. There are also other towering spectacles en route, such as the Eschenheimer Turm, a northern gate tower of the former city fortifications that was built around 1400 by cathedral master builder Madern Gerthener.

The architecture, though, is not what the international community comes for. In fact, it is the spectacular indoor finish that has made the Frankfurt Marathon something of a legend.

RACE DETAILS

WHEN? October
WHEN TO APPLY: By July
HOW MANY TAKE PART? 21,000
DIFFICULTY RATING: 4/10
SPECIAL CONSIDERATIONS: There is a 6¼-hour cutoff time, which might put off those who are unsure about their performance.

CONTACT:
BMW Frankfurt Marathon
Eurocity Marathon, Messe Frankfurt
60135 Frankfurt am Main, Germany
☎ +49 69 3700 4680
✉ mail@frankfurt-marathon.com
🖥 www.bmw-frankfurt-marathon.com

RACE DETAILS

WHEN? September
WHEN TO APPLY: By January
HOW MANY TAKE PART? 4,000
DIFFICULTY RATING: 9/10
SPECIAL CONSIDERATIONS: It is a marathon for the serious contender, and unless you have superhero fitness, you'll be walking for many of the final stretches. Despite this, there is a 6½-hour cutoff time. Mountain terrain. Water and refreshments are in plentiful supply.

CONTACT:
Jungfrau-Marathon Incoming Office
Strandbadstrasse 44
CH-3800 Interlaken
Switzerland
☎ +41 33 827 62 90
✉ info@jungfrau-marathon.ch
🖥 www.jungfrau-marathon.ch

Jungfrau Marathon |
Switzerland

Jungfrau is a mountain race for the seriously committed, where every mile or so the challenge changes, with increasingly steep gradients to be tackled as you gain altitude and lose oxygen. Rising to the challenge pays off with great views and the unparalleled feeling of achievement in making it to the finish line.

The event is as much about climbing as it is about running. The race centers around the Kleine Scheidegg, a mountain pass that rises 6,762 feet (2,061 m) above the Swiss town of Interlaken. The first 15½ miles (25 km) are on relatively flat ground and the going is good, but it is in the last 10½ miles (17 km) where the real climbing begins, and your willpower is tested. Those who rush into an early lead might never make it to the end; it is all about pacing and stamina.

WHILE YOU'RE THERE

Jungfrau's nearest town is **Interlaken**,which is small enough to get around on foot or bike and is a great holiday destination for exploring the **Bernese Oberland**. It is also served by trains to Zurich or Geneva if you want a more metropolitan fix. The town is great for shopping for Swiss souvenirs. For health spa enthusiasts the **Bödelibad Interlaken** has a great sauna, steam bath, and whirlpool. See: www.myswitzerland.com

There are organizations and competitors worldwide who are dedicated to the art of mountain running, and the usual victors of this race are these mountain-running specialists, like the multiple world champion Jonathan Wyatt from New Zealand. To make the finishing line, the winners have to complete the 26.2-mile (42.2 km) course with a significant number of grueling climbs and increases in altitude. It is a bit like a pedestrian version of a mountain stage of the Tour de France, complete with surprisingly strong crowd support along the way.

As many as 4,000 runners from more than 50 countries rise to the challenge of this marathon each year. Many are drawn by the views – a panorama of snow-capped mountains remains in sight at all times, offering a constant reminder of the kind of terrain that is in store.

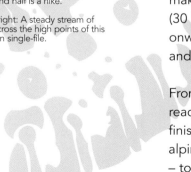

Previous page: The spectacular scenery is a delightful bonus in this tough marathon.

Above: The ascents in the Jungfrau Marathon follow a steep gradient, with climbs from the valley bottom to 5,900 feet (1,800 m).

Top right: Even seasoned marathon runners describe this event as a race of two halves: the first half is a run and the second half is a hike.

Bottom right: A steady stream of runners cross the high points of this scenic run single-file.

Runners pass through Interlaken and then run alongside the wide, refreshing expanse of Lake Brienz and through mountain villages where crowds enthusiastically applaud the runners. It is smooth going as runners pass onward to the magnificence of the Staubbach Falls, but after 15½ miles (25 km), the mountain rises up, and the grueling fight begins. You must make it up 26 sharp mountain bends before reaching 18½ miles (30 km), where music and a cheering crowd help to spur runners onward up the final inclines, beyond the tops of the ski slopes and above the tree line.

From here runners head on to the foot of the Eiger Glacier and reach the highest point of the race at 6,500 feet (2,000 m). The finish lies just beyond, from where there is a view of the high alpine peaks, reminding runners why they came in the first place – to absorb the natural beauty of glaciers, rivers, and forests, and to stand at the finish feeling like they are on top of the world.

RACE DETAILS

WHEN? Mid-October
WHEN TO APPLY: January to September
HOW MANY TAKE PART? 10,000
DIFFICULTY RATING: 4/10
SPECIAL CONSIDERATIONS: One of the fastest courses on the world circuit. Less drama and challenge compared with other marathons.

CONTACT:
TCS Amsterdam Marathon
c/o Le Champion
PO Box 5029
1802 TA Alkmaar, The Netherlands
☎ +31 72 532 48 49
✉ info@tcsamsterdammarathon.nl
🖳 www.tcsamsterdammarathon.nl

Amsterdam Marathon | Holland

It will come as no surprise that Amsterdam hosts one of the flattest marathon courses in the world. That alone sets it up as a place that attracts runners wanting to beat their personal best; however, there is more to this marathon than just flat spaces.

Amsterdam has been a force in the marathon world since the 1970s, earning itself a place in the rankings of the world's best marathons. It regularly features in the top 10 course selections by elite and social runners alike.

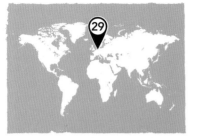

29

WHILE YOU'RE THERE

You can marvel at the masterpieces at the **Van Gogh Museum**, or see other masters such as Matisse and Picasso at the **Stedelijk Museum**.

The **Red Light Distric**t and its paraded wares and peep shows always draws crowds.

One sight visitors never tire of is the maze of canals, each one lined with a myriad of shops, galleries, and authentic cafés.

The most picturesque of canals is **Prinsengracht**, lined by shady trees and colorful houseboats. Here you'll also find **Anne Frank's House**. A well-kept secret worth visiting is Amsterdam's 14th-century garden at **Begijnhof**. See: www.begijnhofamsterdam.nl

Previous page: The marathon route alongside the Amstel River.

Above: The Mizuno Half Marathon Business Run, the Mizuno 5-mile (8 km) run and the ¾-mile (1 km) Olympic Kids Run all take place alongside the main event.

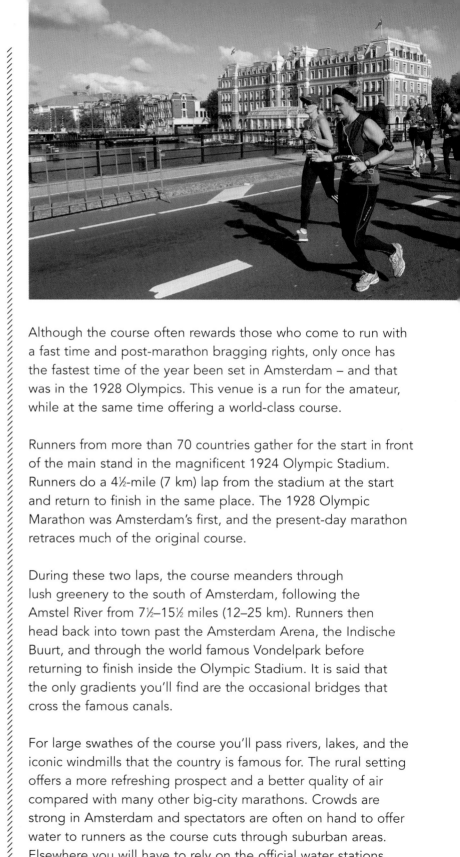

Although the course often rewards those who come to run with a fast time and post-marathon bragging rights, only once has the fastest time of the year been set in Amsterdam – and that was in the 1928 Olympics. This venue is a run for the amateur, while at the same time offering a world-class course.

Runners from more than 70 countries gather for the start in front of the main stand in the magnificent 1924 Olympic Stadium. Runners do a 4½-mile (7 km) lap from the stadium at the start and return to finish in the same place. The 1928 Olympic Marathon was Amsterdam's first, and the present-day marathon retraces much of the original course.

During these two laps, the course meanders through lush greenery to the south of Amsterdam, following the Amstel River from 7½–15½ miles (12–25 km). Runners then head back into town past the Amsterdam Arena, the Indische Buurt, and through the world famous Vondelpark before returning to finish inside the Olympic Stadium. It is said that the only gradients you'll find are the occasional bridges that cross the famous canals.

For large swathes of the course you'll pass rivers, lakes, and the iconic windmills that the country is famous for. The rural setting offers a more refreshing prospect and a better quality of air compared with many other big-city marathons. Crowds are strong in Amsterdam and spectators are often on hand to offer water to runners as the course cuts through suburban areas. Elsewhere you will have to rely on the official water stations.

Rock 'n' Roll Madrid Marathon | Spain

Like many other major city marathons, the Rock 'n' Roll Madrid Marathon was first dreamed up by a group of sports lovers. It took years to sketch plans, organize a route, and turn these dreams into reality. Back in 1978, a marathon was a new idea to the Spanish people, but they have gradually warmed to it and it has become a source of civic pride and a means to project the identity of their city, as happened so poignantly, and with great force, just five weeks after the 2004 Madrid train bombings. Local runners are always a significant presence, but organizers see boosting foreign participation as the key to doubling numbers from the current 10,000 runners to their goal of 20,000.

Madrid lies at an altitude of 2,200 feet (670 m) – enough to make a difference to your likely finishing time. However, the Spanish spring usually offers good running conditions in a city that can, at other times, be hot and humid. In Madrid, locals venture out on a Saturday night no earlier than 10 pm and throng the streets en masse throughout the night with no expectation of returning home until well after sunrise. This social routine works well for the marathon, which then benefits from the relatively empty streets from which runners can strike out on their early-morning mission. The start and finish lie right in the heart of the city, on those just-vacated streets.

From the start line runners tackle a long, gentle incline northward. This is the part of the course on which to relax, mindful that undue effort at even this slight altitude will probably rebound on you later in the race. These early miles are along wide avenues, but bereft of any engaging urban detail. The field of runners thins out slowly, and by the time participants approach the half marathon distance, there is enough room to look around and much to see.

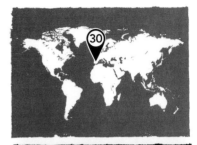

WHILE YOU'RE THERE

For some great sightseeing, go to the Metro by La Latina Station. From there take a stroll around **Plaza de la Cebada**, **Cava Baja**, and **Plaza de la Paja**. After 9 pm the streets slowly come to life. Walk from **el Viaducto Bridge** in the southern limit of La Latina to Plaza España by the **Palacio Real de Madrid**. Alternatively, you can sit and feast at the great tapas bars by **Mercado de San Miguel**.

RACE DETAILS

WHEN? April
WHEN TO APPLY: November of the year before
HOW MANY TAKE PART? 10,000
DIFFICULTY RATING: 7/10
SPECIAL CONSIDERATIONS: Course contains a lot of hills that can challenge the beginner. The city is poised on a dry plain 2,300 feet (700 m) above sea level, so it is best to acclimate to this environment a few days before.

CONTACT:

☎ +858 450 6510 (USA)
✉ rnrmadrid@competitorgroup.com
🖥 www.maratonmadrid.org/

Left: The starting line features marathon runners as well as those taking on the challenge of the 6-mile (10 km) race; the two run simultaneously.

Above: The race is downhill except for two blocks of 4 miles (6 km), each of which includes rather steep climbs.

Right: Madrid is considered a tough marathon with a challenging course, even by seasoned veterans.

Cobbled roads underfoot may inhibit runners from enjoying the surroundings, but there is indeed plenty to see. Competitors sweep into the Puerta del Sol and take a turn past the Plaza Mayor and the Palacio Real. These are the architectural riches of a city that was capital to an empire that covered half the globe. Shortly afterwards, runners experience a contrasting aspect as they descend to the River Manzanares and take in a loop through Madrid's major green space, the Casa de Campo, where all is serene and peaceful, far from the cheering crowd. The other of Madrid's parks, Retiro, is where the race finishes – runners enter through the grand gateway and have an equally grand finishing straight, where spectators bask in the sunshine and await the arrival of their loved ones. In Madrid this usually means the father, as the race is predominantly local and overwhelmingly male. Only 6 percent of the field are women, and this presents the most obvious possible growth area for the future.

Those who run Madrid are drawn back to its espirito de vida. The turnout is impressive, and the support comes with passion and intensity that is both a reflection of its people and a testament to the future of this race.

Paris Marathon | France

Although the Arc de Triomphe was built with another kind of triumphalism in mind, it is a fitting centerpiece that dominates both the start and finish area of the Paris Marathon, reminding the thronging crowds just how big a personal victory running a marathon can be. Just getting to the start line on the Champs-Elysées, with the Arc de Triomphe as a backdrop, represents a victory of sorts – it is one of the few days of the year that the choking Parisian traffic is held at bay for the benefit of the general public. The grand boulevards of Paris unroll in front of the runners, who for the first 1¼ miles (2 km) descend to the Place de La Concorde, and soon afterward reach the Jardin des Tuileries and the Musée du Louvre.

Of the 40,000 runners who take part, more than a quarter come from outside France, from 80 different countries. By far the largest group are the British, who flock to the event under the English Channel on Eurostar trains. In a display of entente cordiale, giant flags line the route – Le Tricolore, the Union Jack, and the Stars and Stripes abound in an explosion of red, white, and blue as if they are welcoming back returning heroes.

In the first Paris Marathon back in 1977, only 87 people finished the race. During the first European running boom of the 1980s, numbers swelled to 7,000, but in 1991 the race was called off due to disputes within the race organization. Since then the Marie de Paris (the city council) has used the Tour de France organizers to stage the race, and it has grown in both size and stature as a result.

The Paris Marathon is central to the city. The start and finish of the race are easily accessed on foot from a host of metro stations, and the course offers a comprehensive tour of the city's sights. If runners have time to glance left as they head down the Rue de Rivoli, they will see the Place Vendôme and the ornate Paris Opera in full view.

WHILE YOU'RE THERE

One of the most charming Parisian districts is **Montmarte**, always full of tourists, but still blessed with a village-like atmosphere. It retains the flavor for which Paris is famous. Packed with cafés and alleys, it is the inspiration for many paintings from the artists who lived there during the 19th and 20th centuries. These include Edgar Degas, Henri Matisse, Henri de Toulouse-Lautrec, Pierre-Auguste Renoir, and Pablo Picasso. Go to Montmarte's famous **cemetery** and you'll see many are buried there. For a more life-affirming experience, **Le Moulin Rouge** still swings to cabaret.

Right: The Paris Marathon offers a scenic route, taking in all the major landmarks of this city – however, bottlenecks can occur.

RACE DETAILS

WHEN? April
WHEN TO APPLY: September of the year before
HOW MANY TAKE PART? Capacity capped at 37,000
DIFFICULTY RATING: 7/10
SPECIAL CONSIDERATIONS: Narrow stretches can lead to running bottlenecks, and the course can become overcrowded. Good crowd support helps considerably to keep the spirit going.

CONTACT:
Amaury Sport Organisation
Immeduble Panorama B
253 Quai de la Bataille de Stalingrad
92137 Issy-les-Moulineaux Cedex
☎ +33 (0)1 41 33 14 00
✉ infos@parismarathon.com
🖥 www.parismarathon.com

The wedding-cake style Hôtel de Ville is a little further along on the right before runners reach the Place de La Bastille. Just beyond, as runners approach the Bois de Vincennes, a giant banner proclaims "Courage: only 20 miles (32 km) to go." After a serpentine tour of the Bois, in which spectators are sparse and the mood almost bucolic, the race passes the halfway point and hits the Rive Droite of the River Seine at 14¼ miles (23 km). The north embankment is not quite flat; runners sometimes get diverted below underpasses in order to avoid closing the bridges down. Surfacing from one such dip, you will catch a glimpse of Notre Dame, then a couple of miles later, at 18 miles (29 km), you emerge to find the Eiffel Tower rearing up on your left-hand side.

The course takes a detour around the Parc des Princes rugby stadium and the Roland Garros tennis clay courts before entering the Bois de Boulogne at 22½ miles (36 km). The last 3¾ miles (6 km) of the course are in the Bois and largely devoid of crowd support. This makes the final 218-yard (200 m) sprint down the Avenue Foch all the more of a climactic moment, and the finish gantry your own personal Arc de Triomphe.

Right: Paris rightly attracts thousands to its marathon, which takes in all the sightseeing scenery that the city has to offer.

Below: Times are not fast for this tricky marathon, and cobblestones add to the challenge for some runners.

RACE DETAILS

WHEN? March
WHEN TO APPLY: By January
HOW MANY TAKE PART? 15,000
DIFFICULTY RATING: 5/10
SPECIAL CONSIDERATIONS: Mild weather conditions at this time of year, low humidity, hills at the beginning and end. Good carnival atmosphere.

CONTACT:
Marató de Barcelona
Gran Via 8-10, 6ª planta
08902 Hospitalet de Llobregat
Barcelona, Spain
☎ +34 902 43 17 63
✉ info@maratobarcelona.es
🖥 www.maratobarcelona.com

Barcelona Marathon | Spain

Hosting the 1992 Olympic Games gave Barcelona an enduring international sporting profile in the world. The Games and their legacy brought a wave of construction to the city's sports facilities and an awareness of how positive energy can renew the spirit of a city and its sports prowess. Having been a recent host to the European Athletics Championship has also helped to improve the infrastructure further, making Barcelona an excellent marathon venue.

The Barcelona Marathon was established in 1978, in a way that has become a familiar model – a Spaniard had run in the New York City Marathon and was so impressed that he returned home to set about creating one in Barcelona. This untried event was then consigned to a route outside town for its inaugural edition to avoid disrupting normal city life, but even so it attracted 1,050 runners, and double that the following year. The course was adapted for the 1980 version when it was held within the city and received far more attention. The race impressed Mayor Pasqual Maragall, who decided to launch an Olympic bid on the back of its success.

In the 1980s Barcelona made some innovations to their marathon that have become part of the modern standard – in 1983 they were the first to introduce dope testing and one of the first to use an electrically powered lead vehicle. Even so, the number of runners only edged up slowly until Olympic year, when 6,000 finished on a tough course that would then be used for the Olympic Marathon a few months later.

After the Olympics, the "Marato," though not the city, slipped back to its former level. Tensions between the club organization and the city authorities eventually led to the cancellation of the 2005 race and the commissioning of the organizers of the Tour de France to stage the 2006 race on a route once again located entirely within the city. Since 2006, entries have risen significantly, surpassing 10,000 in 2010. Foreign runners make up a significant proportion.

Left: A beautiful course with many famous landmarks as well as the Mediterranean sea.

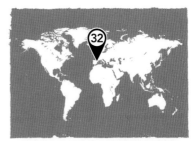

WHILE YOU'RE THERE

It is **Antonio Gaudi's architecture** that many visitors come to see, but few venture out to **Parc Güell**. This is where the artist used to live, and it hosts a wonderland of his more ambitious mosaics and architectural imaginings. The park makes a refreshing alternative to **Las Ramblas**, which has become more of a tourist trap than a place to experience the real Barcelona. The park boasts fairytale sculptures and grand staircases. There is a museum about the life of the man who has become synonymous with the Catalan capital. Also, venture out to the nearby town of **Girona** and its surroundings.

The Marato provides a fitting vehicle through which visitors can catch the sights and sounds of city life that have made Barcelona one of Europe's favorite destinations. Starting at the Plaça d'Espanya, runners pass through the Eixample district and close-by Barcelona Football Club's Camp Nou stadium, the Torre Agbar, Port Olímpic, and along the city's most renowned street, the Ramblas. The stunning architecture of Antonio Gaudi intermittently looms over the route like giant blocks of melted candle wax. The monumental Sagrada Familia cathedral, as well as some smaller apartment buildings, enliven the route with a quirky grandeur.

Barcelona's artisan culture is showcased at 24 different points along the route where music, art, and crafts create a carnival flavor while the race is in full swing. This lends a vibrancy and warmth to a marathon that is rapidly building a following worthily in tune with this iconic city.

Right: The Sagrada Familia cathedral by Gaudi is one of the landmarks of the race.

Below: La Pedrera, a residential building with undulating stone walls and a UNESCO World Heritage Site.

London Marathon | UK

Like many Great British inventions, the London Marathon was dreamt up in a pub over a pint of beer. Athletes and founders Chris Brasher and John Disley modeled it after visiting the New York Marathon in 1979. The festival atmosphere and a route that embraced the key landmarks of one of the world's great cities were essential ingredients. From the launch year in 1981 when 7,000 ran, the participants more than doubled to 16,000 by 1982, making it bigger than the New York event it set out to imitate. Since then, numbers have crept up to 35,000.

Back in the 1970s, long-distance running was a lonely pursuit. Runners were usually consigned to trudging through fields, with only cows as spectators. The London Marathon project aimed to gather these lonely joggers and get them to take part in a celebratory spectacle like that of New York, which had been referred to by Chris Brasher as, "the world's most human race." He explained that what he had seen demonstrated that, "the human race can be one joyous family, working together, laughing together, and achieving the impossible." He and Disley set out to achieve that "impossibility" in London.

33

WHILE YOU'RE THERE

Try some traditional UK carb-laden fare and have some **fish and chips**. A favorite is Poppies, near Spitalfields market; the eatery is decked out in 1950s vintage diner décor, and comes to life late on Sunday evenings. To fit in some sightseeing, one of the quickest ways to see London is to take one of the speedy Clipper river boats that cover many key sites, from **Richmond** to **Big Ben**, as well as the marathon starting point at **Greenwich maritime center**. With a day pass you can hop on and off as many times as you want. See: www.thamesclippers.com and www.thamesflyer.com

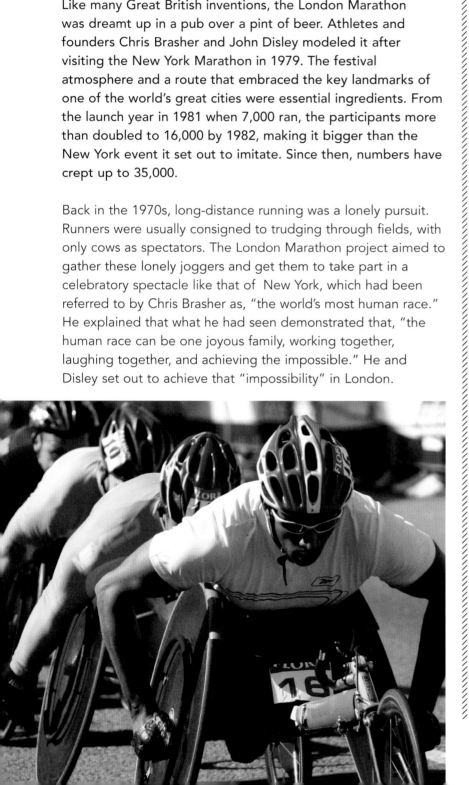

Left: The wheelchair event at the London Marathon attracts a world-class group.

Right: The London Marathon has a fabulous atmosphere as thousands take to the streets to raise money for charities of all kinds.

RACE DETAILS

WHEN? April
WHEN TO APPLY: One year in advance
HOW MANY TAKE PART? 35,000
DIFFICULTY RATING: 5/10
SPECIAL CONSIDERATIONS: The starting point at Greenwich is not the easiest part of the city to get to on a Sunday morning, so factor in time for this. The course can become narrow at times because of the volume of crowds.

CONTACT:
Virgin London Marathon
PO Box 3460,
London
SE1 0YA

☎ +44 (0)20 7902 0200
🖥 www.london-marathon.co.uk

The course has kept to essentially the same route, starting in the ornate gardens and 17th-century grandeur of Greenwich, a host site to events of the 2012 Olympic Games, before dropping down to the River Thames at Woolwich and then turning up river toward Tower Bridge. This iconic Victorian structure is almost at the halfway mark, acting as a gateway to the rest of the course as runners head back down river toward the Canary Wharf business district and many of London's tallest buildings. The course then loops back toward Tower Bridge and the Tower of London and goes on to the Embankment, passing Cleopatra's Needle and reaching Big Ben, from where there is less than 1 mile (1.5 km) to run. The finishing line comes 220 yards (200 m) after runners pass directly in front of Buckingham Palace.

One thing that the founding fathers may not have foreseen was the way in which the London Marathon has become such an effective and high-profile vehicle for charitable fundraising. With the race so over-subscribed, one way of securing a place is to raise funds for a charity that offers guaranteed places. This has generated vast sums (estimated at $80 million each year). It creates a unique atmosphere of cajoling money from bystanders as well as mammoth personal efforts from particpants, who are often dressed in outrageous costumes.

Above: The London Marathon is so over-subscribed that it can take up to six years to secure a place in the ballot. Running for a charity is another way to get you in.

Loch Ness Marathon | Scotland, UK

The Loch Ness Marathon logo, a sinuous shoelace snaking through running shoe eyelets, is worthy of the famous monster it depicts. It is as close as you will come to spotting "Nessie," and the organizers do not attempt to pretend otherwise. Loch Ness, however, has other more tangible attractions.

Inverness is a long way north in Scotland, although its airport has good connections with most UK airports. Perhaps because of this northerly location, the town provides a warm welcome. Part of this involves the local whiskies from which the area derives as much fame as the elusive monster. However, for runners, the most immediate impression is that of the serene landscape. Inverness is an imposing blend of granite brick and modern office blocks, but this is where the race ends – the point-to-point course starts on an appropriately rugged, unadorned stretch of road to which runners are taken by bus on race morning, and which takes on the look of a latter-day gathering of lycra-clad clans.

Belying the serenity of today's quiet glens, clan feuding dominated life here 300 years ago. Inverness was sacked seven times, and Bonnie Prince Charlie's forces were crushed on Culloden Field in the last bloody battle ever fought on British soil. You can now view the site of the famous battle at Culloden Moor Visitors Center. The marathon is a less bloodthirsty affair, but the ambition for victory could be said to be just as strong.

As the dawn light spreads, maybe something of the past can be sensed, but race preparation leaves little time for diversion. The sounds of bagpipes and drums rouse runners to the starting line but, once on the road, the only traffic you're likely to encounter are fellow runners, red squirrels, deer, and eagles. The course begins by passing through farmland on side roads before steering toward the side of the Loch. The route drops from start to finish, although there are also some uphill sections. The first 6 miles (10 km) are gentle, sheltered by woods with scenic views regularly opening up across the Loch. Villages and spectators dot the route, offering refreshments to the weary.

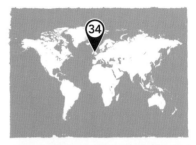

WHILE YOU'RE THERE

You won't have time to take in the full beauty of **Loch Ness** during the marathon. Take a cruise along the Loch and stop off at **Urquhart Castle** while you're touring. The edifice makes an imposing backdrop to this corner of the lake. Further afar you're in the prime vicinity to take some **whisky distillery tours**, many of which offer free tastings. The nearby town of **Inverness** makes a great spot for an afternoon stroll. See www.visitscotland.com and www.spiritofspeyside.com

RACE DETAILS

WHEN? October
WHEN TO APPLY: By July
HOW MANY TAKE PART? 8,500
DIFFICULTY RATING: 5/10
SPECIAL CONSIDERATIONS: The race takes place in one of Scotland's mountainous regions, so be prepared for steep ascents. Because of the nature of the course, there are few spectators.

CONTACT:
Loch Ness Marathon
PO Box 26
Muir of Ord
IV6 7WZ
UK
☎ +44 844 875 1411
✉ info@lochnessmarathon.com
🖥 www.lochnessmarathon.com

Organizers have strategically placed lone bagpipers in places where they suspect morale might flag, for example, once runners have left the Loch behind and head toward the town. Once the River Ness Bridge has been crossed and runners turn back around along the river, they are likely to be able to sense the finish. Long-term sponsor, Baxter's Foods, offers participants hearty Scottish fare to replenish marathon finishers once they reach the race end in the town stadium.

Between the natural scenery, clean fresh air, and warmth of the local hospitality, it is not so surprising that this relatively secluded corner of the British Isles attracts a sell-out field, with runners coming from 30 countries for a chance to race in this remote, romantic Highland location. Off the track, the Loch Ness area is one of Europe's richest areas for natural bounty, thriving with exotic birds, red deer, and the humble goat. One of its most recent additions is the opening of the South Loch Ness walking trail, which helps visitors see some of the best points of the loch that have not been open before.

Sahara Marathon | Algeria

To run through territory as forbidding as the Sahara requires a certain resolve, but that pales into insignificance compared to what lies behind the creation of this event. The race was conceived as a humanitarian initiative to raise awareness of living conditions in the Western Sahara. Marathon participants discover these easily enough: for several days they are billeted in refugee camps within the homes of the displaced Sahrawi and, as a result, discover the culture around them.

RACE DETAILS

WHEN? October
WHEN TO APPLY: Preparations and applications should be made one year in advance
HOW MANY TAKE PART? 400
DIFFICULTY RATING: 9/10
SPECIAL CONSIDERATIONS: Like no other marathon, so throw away all preconceptions. Running through the desert can be testing, but there are plenty of water stations, and the crowd support is great at stopover camps, not to mention the hospitality.

CONTACT:

✉ rmdurli@saharawi.org
🖥 www.saharamarathon.org (the website includes contacts for individual countries)

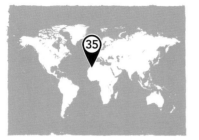

35

WHILE YOU'RE THERE

The race takes place near the town of **Tindouf**, well worth exploring for its friendly faces, camels, and whitewashed street buildings. The desert's cape is also good for photography and the more adventurous pastime of **jeep overlanding**, A word of caution, however; always go with a trusted guide, as landmines pose a threat, as well as the danger of being in the desert too long. Many marathon runners stay **in the camps** with the friends they have made on the way, once the race is over.

After the death of General Franco in 1975, and the sudden Spanish withdrawal from the territory formerly known as Spanish Sahara, a struggle began between the Sahrawi people and the neighboring states of Mauritania and Morocco. A guerrilla war dragged on for years, but eventually 80,000 Sahrawi were driven into four refugee camps over the border in the Algerian desert near Tindouf. During 30 years of deprivation, disease, and severely hostile conditions, the refugees formed the Sahrawi Arab Democratic Republic (SADR). They developed a highly structured government system in the camps to manage their scarce resources. All of this was achieved with little support from western governments, but one group that did help was the US Western Sahara Foundation. Jeb Carney, a board member of the foundation and a marathon runner, led a delegation to the camps in 1999. The idea of running a marathon between the camps was developed as a means of increasing awareness of the Sahrawi plight and their efforts to build a civil society.

Previous page: Hard-packed sand is a runner-friendly surface – only when the wind gusts does it present real difficulty.

Above: The Sahara Marathon demands greater participation of its runners than most marathons. The 500 entrants stay as guests in the tents of the Sahrawi people for one week.

Top right: A children's race follows the marathon.

Bottomt right: This is a desert run where conditions can be extreme.

The basic idea was simple and, due to the willingness of the Sahrawi, immediately effective. The course was marked out using cairns, or stacks of stones, to guide runners over the open desert between the three refugee camps of El Aaiún, El Aoserd, and Smara, each named after an equivalent settlement in Western Sahara. The first marathon was held on February 26, 2001, the 25th anniversary of the founding of SADR.

The first two years of the Sahara Marathon brought in more than 900 runners from 30 countries on charter flights, revealing a glimpse of life in the Sahara that would change their perception of the Sahrawi forever. Participants are hosted during their stay by Sahrawi families, living in their tents and eating with them, experiencing their life and the harsh conditions in the camps. It is a chance to share part of their life, to learn about them, and to create ties that in many cases last for years, with some runners returning every year to run and to see their host families and friends again.

Reykjavik Marathon | Iceland

Iceland is far from being the forbidding place that its name might suggest. The Icelandic summer is short, but it offers relatively mild and breezy weather. This, along with often flat, well-surfaced roads and a sparse population, makes it an almost idyllic setting for distance running.

Like the town itself, the Reykjavik Marathon lives up to its reputation of being intimate and unpretentious. People often describe the capital as a cosmopolitan city crammed into the form of a fishing village. When the marathon first started, just 214 competitors signed up, but that is something that distinguishes this country from anywhere else — life is lived on a smaller (and arguably a more comfortable) scale. The same applies to its marathon. The population of Iceland is a mere 320,000, so anything that attracts overseas visitors usually gains the support of the Icelanders. In their own unfussy way they are very welcoming people.

The focal point of the marathon and the concurrently run half marathon is a picturesque pond called Tjörnin, just outside the city center on which the Reykjavik City Hall is located. This idyllic setting is a haven full of birdlife and fringed with the distinctive wooden houses that characterize Icelandic domestic architecture. The run begins and ends here, but it embraces quite another world in between.

Runners leave the center almost as soon as they depart from the start line, threading their way through the suburban surroundings and onto the Reykjavik peninsula's coastal path. The imposing green bulk of Mount Esja dominates the landscape from across the bay, still crowned by remnants of snow. Runners turn back toward the city center, along a route lapped by a geothermally heated beach, another of Iceland's natural wonders.

The natural environment wonderfully complements the running experience in Iceland. Reykjavik translates as "smoky bay," even though there is no smoke or pollution.

WHILE YOU'RE THERE

The **fishing harbors** are a great place to pick up the latest fresh fish dish. Near the capital there are a myriad of **natural thermal springs**, heated by the underlying thermal rock, making a great antidote to aches and pains resulting from a hard run. The most famous and accessible from the capital is the **Blue Lagoon**. Its springs are made of seawater that come from deep within the earth, capturing minerals that result in bathing waters of around 98°F (37°C) that are renowned for their healing powers. See: ww.bluelagoon.com

Right: Marathoners and half marathoners run the same race, with those doing the shorter distance branching off at 12 miles (19 km).

The ancient Viking name refers to the geothermal steam that mysteriously seeps out of the ground. Nonetheless, the air quality is the best in Europe, so visiting runners can breathe easily. They can also enjoy a long, relaxing post-race soak in one of Iceland's many geothermal pools. One of them, the Blue Lagoon, lies en route to Keflavik International Airport.

Making it to Iceland is an adventure in itself, even if you don't run the marathon. The participants from Europe and North America and beyond have saved money, begged for charity donations, and trained hard to be here. You can feel that such investment energizes and enthuses the crowd as the starting gun fires.

One reason why the Reykjavik Marathon has become such a big event is that it coincides with "Culture Night," which was created to celebrate the best Icelandic traditions including music, art, and gourmet whaleshark meat-tasting sessions. The program of events includes string quartets, art exhibits, and theater, while the crowd is a heady mix of graffiti artists and those wearing rock outfits. The marathon after-party culminates with a mammoth firework display, which is the cue to head for the city's clubs and bars. Still riding high from the euphoria of the marathon, participants throw themselves into the all-night party.

RACE DETAILS

WHEN? Mid-August
WHEN TO APPLY: January to May
HOW MANY TAKE PART? 10,000
DIFFICULTY RATING: 6/10
SPECIAL CONSIDERATIONS: Iceland is famed for its clean and fresh air. It has one of the smallest populations of any country in the world, so don't expect huge crowds if that is what drives you.

CONTACT:
Engjavegir 6
104 Reykjavík
Iceland
☎ +354 535 3700 and 535 3702
✉ marathon@marathon.is
💻 www.marathon.is

RACE DETAILS

WHEN? July
WHEN TO APPLY: January
HOW MANY TAKE PART? 4,000
DIFFICULTY RATING: 6/10
SPECIAL CONSIDERATIONS: Flat course, so don't expect huge challenges. The traffic can be daunting for some.

CONTACT:
Rua Felix Pacheco 150 Bldg C Apt. 102
Leblon 22450 080, Brazil
☎ +21 22 23 2273
✉ maratonadorio@
maratonadorio.com.br
🖥 www.maratonadorio.com.br

Rio de Janeiro Marathon | Brazil

Rio de Janeiro's marathon follows a point-to-point route starting from the western edge of town at Recreio dos Bandeirantes, a strip of development lying between the beach and the inland lagoons and marshes. Runners follow the coast all the way into the city center. Half marathon runners start closer to town, at São Conrado. It is after this point that runners encounter a sustained rise, as the road climbs around a rocky headland on Oscar Niemeyer Drive. To the right, runners can gaze out over the brilliant blue of the South Atlantic Ocean, while a steep tree-covered cliff rises up on their other side. Around the headland, the road drops back down to beach level about 15½ miles (25 km) into the race, and on the beaches themselves, Brazilian life is all around to see.

Brazilians treat the beach like people elsewhere would a park, coming to play chess, football, or volleyball, or to chat and meet up with friends – anything rather than just lie around. Each beach has its own distinctive character – upscale Leblon, fashionable Ipanema, and popular Copacabana.

Brazil is a country where the spirit of participation is infectious: rogue roller bladers, cyclists, and pedestrians will try to join in the marathon. To stop them from becoming too involved, a lead flotilla of cars and security bikes steer them away and the sound of their sirens clears a path for the oncoming leaders of the race. This happens twice in succession, as Brazilian races commonly feature a separate start for the faster women ahead of the mass field, so that leading women can focus on the competition.

From the moment runners reach Leblon, the road is flat and the running becomes easy. After the beaches, the route heads inland, cutting through a tunnel to Botafogo Bay. With no attached beach, crowds are small here as runners sweep around the bay under the shadow of the Sugar Loaf Mountain toward Flamengo Beach. Runners stay on the highway inland from the beach park, turning at the far end and doubling back to the finish line. It has been a long journey to get here, and even on this midwinter date in mid-July, the day is bound to be hot. However, the beach is nearby.

WHILE YOU'RE THERE

There are few better ways to soak up the native **Carioca** lifestyle than an afternoon on the beach – it is where Brazilian social life is in full force. The more fashionable sands are at **Leblon** or **Ipanema**, rather than **Copacabana**.
The **Christ the Redeemer** statue is a must-visit, as is the **Sugar Loaf Mountain**.
If you're in need of a post-marathon feast, head to a **churrascaria** (steakhouse), such as Parcão Rio (www.porcao.com.br); hunks of prime steak will be carved onto your plate. There is an amazing salad bar, too, packed with exotic fruit and salads.
If you have a week or more, head to the retreat of **Búzios**, with 30 beaches to choose from.

Left: Spectacular scenery offers a superb backdrop to the physical efforts of the runners.

Run Barbados Marathon | Barbados

"Come for the run, stay for the fun" is the invitation put out by the Barbados Tourism Authority to attract runners to race on this most open of Caribbean islands. The lure of beach parties and calypso may be ever-present, but the Barbados Race Series has hosted many a serious athlete, including Olympic medalists, since it started in 1983.

The sun is usually what draws visitors to the island, but when it comes to the race, all efforts are in place to avoid it. The marathon starts at 4:30 am, it gets light at 5:40 am, and less than an hour later it already feels hot. Even though midday temperatures are not often greater than 86°F (30°C), the direct sun beating down takes its toll.

The race starts on the Bay Street Esplanade, just outside the Prime Minister's office on the south side of Bridgetown. Running in the pre-dawn darkness through the empty shuttered streets of Bridgetown has a slightly eerie feel. Even when you have passed the harbor and are heading north on the Spring Garden Highway alongside the beach at 3 miles (5 km), the only audible sounds are the breathing and footfall of fellow runners (unless, that is, you are close enough to the front to hear the pounding bass of the speakers on the support vehicle accompanying the leaders). The course clings closely to the shoreline, so it remains level for the most part. However, in a couple of places – around the contrasting sites of the Esso refinery at 3¾ miles (6 km) and again at the opulent Sandy Lane Hotel after 7 miles (11 km) – it diverts inland a little up an incline before reverting to the shoreline, backing palm-fringed, white-sand beaches.

The sense of detachment only lessens after reaching the residential areas, where women in nightgowns, up early to get Sunday lunch on the go before attending church, appear in front gardens to make comments and hand out cups of water where needed. The morning peals of bells wafting from the open shutters of churches on the way up the west coast offer a spiriting lift to weary runners. The views are varied – sometimes out to sea across a slither of white sand, and sometimes past roadside shops and houses with banana palms, breadfruit trees,

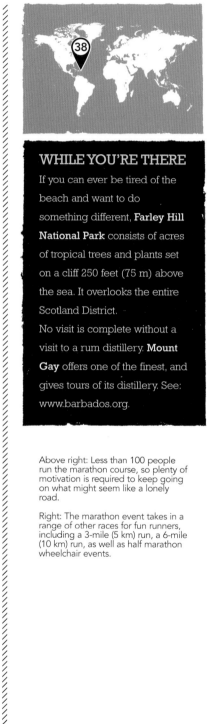

WHILE YOU'RE THERE

If you can ever be tired of the beach and want to do something different, **Farley Hill National Park** consists of acres of tropical trees and plants set on a cliff 250 feet (75 m) above the sea. It overlooks the entire Scotland District.

No visit is complete without a visit to a rum distillery. **Mount Gay** offers one of the finest, and gives tours of its distillery. See: www.barbados.org.

Above right: Less than 100 people run the marathon course, so plenty of motivation is required to keep going on what might seem like a lonely road.

Right: The marathon event takes in a range of other races for fun runners, including a 3-mile (5 km) run, a 6-mile (10 km) run, as well as half marathon wheelchair events.

bougainvillea, and vividly variegated croton hedges busting out from every spare bit of earth. After the tiny fish market in Paynes Bay, where the half marathon runners make their turn, marathon runners pass on beyond Sandy Lane to Holetown, where settlers landed in 1627, and which is now the main tourist center on the sheltered west coast. It is another 3¾ miles (6 km) before runners reach Speightstown, first set up as a trading post in 1630, and ¾ mile (1 km) beyond that before they make the turn and head back toward Bridgetown. This is one of the points on the course where the warm waters of the Caribbean Sea are almost lapping at runners' feet. These are once again appreciated on the return journey, at Mullins, at Paynes Bay, and along the Spring Garden Highway, because it is light and hot, and runners are desperate to submerge themselves in the sea's cooling embrace.

There is a tough section back through the harbor and town before crossing Independence Bridge and hitting Bay Street, tracing the sweeping curve of Bridgetown's Carlisle Bay. Toward the end of it, the Esplanade comes into view and runners cross the finish line and walk around the back of the bandstand and into those inviting waters.

RACE DETAILS

WHEN? December
WHEN TO APPLY: By October
HOW MANY TAKE PART? 700
DIFFICULTY RATING: 7/10
SPECIAL CONSIDERATIONS: Early 4:30 am start, but still prepare for heat and humidity. Lonely in many stretches, but the pristine beach is the big payoff. Keep an open mind; it is not as organized as many marathons.

CONTACT:
Barbados Tourism Authority
PO Box 246 Harbour Road
Bridgetown, Barbados
☎ +246 467 3660
✉ angelaw@visitbarbados.org
🖥 www.runbarbados.org

Boston Marathon | USA

The Boston Marathon is the oldest annual marathon in the world, having been run continuously since 1897, the year after the first Modern Olympics of 1896, for which the modern marathon was invented. Back then there were just 18 people running. During the centenary edition in 1996, more than 35,000 people ran. The 1996 marathon was the first to see such a high number of runners. In fact, in that year people did not have to run a qualifying time to be accepted. Usually, in order to qualify, every runner must have finished a certified marathon within a specified (fast) time dependent on the age of the runner. The qualifying standard is high enough to make qualifying for Boston – also known as "to BQ" – an achievement in itself.

The Boston Marathon for many years fell short of the marathon distance. In 1907, the start was moved west from Ashland to Hopkinton, but the distance remained no more than 24½ miles (39 km) until 1924, and even between 1951 and 1956 it was only 25 miles (40.5 km). The route travels east and gently downhill for the first half, but then drops more sharply until reaching the famous four Newton Hills, among which lies so-called "heartbreak hill." This hill does not, as one may think, get its name from runners heartbroken because they have to conquer yet another ascent, but the name does originate in the Boston Marathon. The story relates that during the 1936 race, defending champion John A. Kelley caught up with race leader Ellison "Tarzan" Brown, giving him a consolatory pat on the shoulder as he overtook him. This overbearing gesture apparently riled Tarzan sufficiently, and he went on to retake the lead and win the race. In the words of a local journalist, the bitter defeat "broke Kelley's heart."

From here, the course again gently descends to the finish in the center of Boston. Overall the course drops 440 feet (135 m) from start to finish, or 10¾ feet (3.3 m) for every ¾ mile (1 km) of its length. This gravitational advantage for runners is

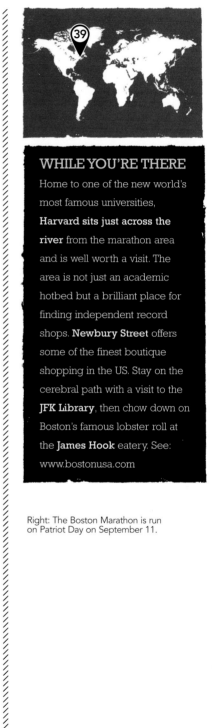

WHILE YOU'RE THERE

Home to one of the new world's most famous universities, **Harvard sits just across the river** from the marathon area and is well worth a visit. The area is not just an academic hotbed but a brilliant place for finding independent record shops. **Newbury Street** offers some of the finest boutique shopping in the US. Stay on the cerebral path with a visit to the **JFK Library**, then chow down on Boston's famous lobster roll at the **James Hook** eatery. See: www.bostonusa.com

Right: The Boston Marathon is run on Patriot Day on September 11.

RACE DETAILS

WHEN? April
WHEN TO APPLY: Applications open for a limited time in September before the marathon
HOW MANY TAKE PART? 35,000
DIFFICULTY RATING: 6/10
SPECIAL CONSIDERATIONS: Inhospitable hills, but a warm atmosphere. You have to qualify before you take part. Great support from crowds and fellow runners.

CONTACT:
Boston Athletic Association
40 Trinity Place
4th Floor Boston
MA02116, USA
☎ +1 617 236 1652
✉ info@baa.org
🖥 www.baa.org/races/boston-marathon.aspx

on occasion supplemented by an assisting wind. Such was the case in 1994, when Cosmas Ndeti won, and again in 2011, when a strong tailwind helped to push Geoffrey Mutai to the fastest time ever run over the marathon distance, at 2:03:02. The time cannot be recognized as a record (in fact, no times recorded in Boston can) because of the advantages afforded by overall gradient and wind direction.

In most years Boston has not produced particularly fast times, perhaps partly because the general rhythm of running downhill for the first 15½ miles (25 km) is disturbed by the following uphill section. At other times, the adversity of the conditions, varying from freezing rain to boiling heat, is a factor that can affect times significantly. What the race has produced are a number of thrillingly competitive duels, such as Bill Rodgers against Jeff Wells 1978, and Alberto Salazar against Dick Beardsley in 1982. In recent years, it has been the elite women, who start separately before the mass race, who have given Boston's avid marathon aficionados the most dramatic denouements.

Below: Everyone who runs the Boston Marathon has to qualify by running another marathon in a fast time.

ING New York City Marathon | USA

Just like anything in the Big Apple, this race is on a monumental scale; it is the biggest marathon there is, with upwards of 45,000 runners taking part.

New York staged the first marathon in the Western Hemisphere in September 1896, soon after the Athens Olympics, but, unlike the Boston race that was held six months later, it did not survive. New York reestablished a marathon in 1970. Fred Lebow, originally from Romanian Transylvania, worked in the New York rag trade when he organized a marathon of four laps entirely within Central Park. It was a low-key affair, with each runner paying a modest $1 entry fee. Just 55 of the 127 entrants finished the race.

It was not until the 1976 race, which coincided with the American Bicentennial, that things took off, and the New York Marathon was reinvented as the model for all other mass marathons. It started with a suggestion from Ted Corbett, a well-known local runner, to invite teams from the five boroughs of the city to compete in the race. Somehow, City Hall interpreted this as a citywide race through the five boroughs – and they jumped on the idea. Lebow was against this at first, seeing the logistical problems more clearly than city officials.

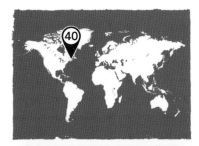

WHILE YOU'RE THERE

In New York City, the options on tours are seemingly limitless. Take a **pizza tour of Brooklyn**; a tour of **gangster sites in New York**; a **tour of film locations**; a **hip hop tour of Harlem**; even a rather gruesome tour of where famous people have died. There are also plenty of transportation options – walking, biking, subway or the ubiquitous yellow taxi. For post-marathon hunger pangs, one of the favorite spots for locals is **Shake Shack**, with many locations across NYC, including a new one in Battery Park City. See: www.nycgo.com

Left: The New York City Marathon has a competitive field for wheelchair races.

A new route transformed the old race and introduced a new starting point on Staten Island at the iconic Verazzano Bridge. No longer confined within Central Park, people could not help but pay attention when the marathon went through main-city thoroughfares. People relished the chance to run in such a public spectacle, and entries poured in until the 2,100 cap set that year was reached. In subsequent years the entries rapidly escalated, reaching 14,000 by 1979.

The course offers a sightseeing tour as well as a sporting event, traveling through parts of the city that many tourists would never see. It offers awe-inspiring views of New York Harbor, the Statue of Liberty, and Lower Manhattan, as well as a tough but exhilarating climb over the 59th Street Bridge. On reaching Manhattan, runners take a long northward turn up First Avenue to the Bronx, before doubling back to the Central Park finish by way of Harlem and Fifth Avenue.

Most events, dwarfed by the sheer size of the city, struggle to capture the imagination of the average New Yorker.

Above: Many runners report that this marathon is an unforgettable experience, with flawless organization and energetic public support.

RACE DETAILS

WHEN? November
WHEN TO APPLY: November of the year before
HOW MANY TAKE PART? 45,000
DIFFICULTY RATING: 6/10
SPECIAL CONSIDERATIONS: Early morning start in November means the weather can be very chilly, so pack the thermals. Lots of inclines and bridges, as well as masses of people; it can get crowded, especially at the start. Give yourself plenty of time to get there.

CONTACT:
ING New York City Marathon
New York Road Runners
9 East 89th Street
New York, NY 10128, USA
☎ +212 423 2249
✉ marathonmailer@nyrr.org
🖥 www.ingnycmarathon.org

Above: Moral support is provided all the way around this course.

Marathon day is different. On the first Sunday of November, New Yorkers stop what they are doing and come out to cheer on the runners. More than 100 live bands play along the course, turning the event into a mini carnival.

Each year 100,000 people apply to take one of the 45,000 places on offer. Organizers charge a hefty premium to overseas tour operators for allotted places, knowing that the appeal of this run can readily pry open runners' purses.

In 1976, the organizers of the New York Marathon created a template for every modern marathon. The race was no longer just about finding a loop in which to cover the required distance; it became a way to unite a city, allowing participants to take a grand tour of New York and experience something truly magical. This spirit lives on in the modern race and has ignited a passion for marathon running that has spread around the globe. Just as a debt is owed to the original Athens Marathon, so too must the vision of the New York Marathon organizers be appreciated by every marathon enthusiast.

Marine Corps Marathon | USA

The Marine Corps Marathon styles itself as "The People's Race," relying on the appreciation of ordinary runners rather than trying to entice an elite field – unusually, there is no prize money offered. Since the 9/11 tragedy in 2001, running this most patriotic of American marathons has often been undertaken as a mark of respect to those who have been victims of war, whether civilians or those in the armed forces.

Of the 30,000 participants who enter each year – and places are usually snapped up within a few hours of the online entry opening – an average of 40 percent are attempting their first marathon. The race is for the glory of running itself, with participants drawn by the smooth, flat surface of the course, and the chance to tour the US capital.

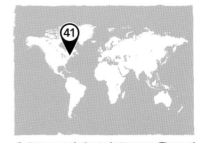

WHILE YOU'RE THERE

The Marine Corps Marathon takes place in the capital. While it might not have the buzz of New York, it is overflowing with famous landmarks, such as **The White House**, **Capitol Hill**, and the **Lincoln Memorial**. Abraham Lincoln is probably one president you'll want to see while in the city – his monument is more like a temple, adorned with 36 Doric columns, and is at the heart of the main attractions. Washington is also home to the **Smithsonian**, the world's largest museum complex.

Left: The Marine Corps Marathon is a race that embodies pure, unashamed patriotism.

Right: The landmarks are just one part of the appeal of this marathon: many US citizens run it as a way to publicly support the work of the US troops.

WHEN? October
WHEN TO APPLY: One year in advance
HOW MANY TAKE PART? 30,000
DIFFICULTY RATING: 5/10
SPECIAL CONSIDERATIONS: A race for first-timers, but more tough than you'd expect with inclines, hills, and a bridge. There are reports of crowding on public transportation before and after the race, so plan time around this.

CONTACT:
Marine Corps Marathon
PO Box 188
Quantico, VA 22134, USA
☎ 1-800-RUN USMC
✉ marine.marathon@usmc.mil
🖳 www.marinemarathon.com

The race starts with the national anthem, pledging allegiance to the flag, and a flurry of star-spangled banners waving in the autumnal light. It is an inclusive sort of patriotism, as plenty of non-US runners are among the crowd, waving flags from their home nations. A supersonic flyover of F/A-18 Hornet attack fighter jets and CH-53 Sea Stallion helicopters makes a suitably dramatic opening to this great race.

The course meanders around the lower reaches of the Potomac River, with the topographical high points coming at 3 miles (5 km) and 8 miles (13 km), but all the major sights are saved for much later in the race at 15½–20 miles (25–32 km). At this point, runners circumnavigate the Reflecting Pool, pass by the Lincoln Memorial and then along Constitution Avenue with the White House and the Washington Memorial to each side, followed by the museums, the Grant Memorial, and finally the Capitol. After this touristic tour de force, runners cross back over the Potomac for the final couple of miles (few kilometers), passing the Pentagon and reaching the Iwo Jima Memorial at the finish line.

Even without considering the monuments, the city appears at its best at the time of the race, with the vivid autumnal colors.

Above: The race provides the occasion to revel in the military pride of the US and the service given by the country's combat forces, their friends, and families.

Reggae Marathon | Jamaica

The Reggae marathon is a carnival, a food festival, and a music extravaganza all in one. Organizers aim to attract runners from all over the world to sample what they call "running in paradise." This world event started on a local footing with a loose collection of runners gathering at Kingston's reservoir, nicknamed "The Dam." They formed a club called the "Jamdammers" in 1995, and to celebrate their fifth birthday the Reggae Marathon was born. Now into its second decade, the Reggae Marathon has its own unique character.

The race name is not surprising considering Jamaica was the birthplace of Reggae music legend Bob Marley. Such is his legacy that Marley's sons have run this race, but the course is as much of an attraction as the music. The Reggae Marathon takes place on the first Saturday in December and starts in the dark at 5:15 am, when it is what the locals call "chilly," but which those from cooler climes might consider as balmy. Chilly, in the context of a Jamaican winter, means about 77°F (25°C). When the sun rises (just a couple of hours after the start of the race), the temperature rises to 90°F (32°C).

Below: The local people turn out in force to support the runners of this appealing marathon.

Preceding the marathon is what's billed as the best pasta party in the world, with plenty of dishes with a distinct, local flavor. On race day itself, a flaming tiki (bamboo) torch procession lends an almost mystical quality to the scene as runners gather at the start line, which is enhanced by the unmistakable Caribbean sound of Rasta drummers. Runners head south along Long Bay to the Negril Roundabout, where they then turn back to return to the start.

The 6-mile (10 km) runners stop here, but the half marathon runners go on to a second turning point at the other end of Long Bay before returning. Marathon runners go further along the scenic coast road, with beaches to the left and marshland called the "Great Morass" to the right. Several of the place names here – Bloody Bay and Crocodile Rock, for example – sound as if they have come directly from a pirate captain's treasure map.

WHILE YOU'RE THERE

Jamaica may seem like it is packed with tourists, but there are still many hidden gems to explore. The beaches are a given; among the most loved by locals is **Dr's Cove**. The **Blue Mountains** are best known for coffee and are good for hiking and wildlife trails. There is also **Golden Eye**, the home of Bond writer Ian Fleming, with the island often used as a location for 007 films. See: www.visitjamaica.com.

Left: The races in this series start at Long Bay Beach Resort, halfway along the 7-mile (11 km) white-sand beach.. It's an early start for the competitors to make the best of the cool morning.

Below: The leaders in the field will be home and finished before the day has started for most people.

Along with the impressive natural scenery comes the manmade enhancements of sound systems, DJ booths, and cars with speakers strapped to the roof, pumping out bass. The wayside crowds are also on hand to lend their support. This can vary from spraying water, handing out bottles of energy drinks, or blasting their own reggae classics to keep the rhythm alive.

Barbecue smoke wafts from the finishing line as the race seamlessly moves into one big after-party, featuring the latest reggae acts and a full Jamaican menu of jerk chicken and curry goat with rice and peas. A post-marathon breakfast is offered in the appropriately named town of Margaritaville. Just make sure you cross the finish line before you go there.

RACE DETAILS

WHEN? First Saturday in December
WHEN TO APPLY: November
HOW MANY TAKE PART? 1,500
DIFFICULTY RATING: 7/10
SPECIAL CONSIDERATIONS: The race starts in the dark in the early morning in order to take advantage of cooler temperatures. Limited visibility until the sun rises and high temperatures when it does are both things to watch.

CONTACT:
Reggae Marathon Ltd
87–89 Tower Street
Kingston, Jamaica

☎ +876 922 8677
🖥 www.reggaemarathon.com

Toronto Waterfront Marathon | Canada

With three of the biggest marathon courses in North America – New York, Boston, and Chicago – on its doorstep, Toronto might well have been forgiven if it had hosted a lesser event. But this marathon, like those of other major cities, confidently attracts elite runners to its international-standard course.

The reason is Lake Ontario. There is an undeniable something about running beside the water, and Toronto took that idea and ran with it – in fact all 26.2 miles (42.2 km) that make up the course of the Scotiabank Toronto Waterfront Marathon overlook the water.

Toronto has another card to play. Surprising as it may seem, the United Nations declares the Canadian metropolis to be the most ethnically diverse city in the world, with almost half of its population coming from outside Canada's borders. Runners from all parts of the world can feel at home here. Nationalities that would declare themselves sworn enemies in other parts of the world seem to find common ground in Toronto. The race celebrates such diversity by deliberately steering a course through 10 different ethnic districts, each with their own style of celebrating the marathon. Runners go through Little Poland, Little Italy, and toward the Caribbean, and then encounter the colorful costumes of Little India. Bollywood beats then set the racing rhythm onward to Little Asia, where 16 bands play, successfully elevating the running spirit.

This race started life as a half marathon in 1990 and after some success was extended to full marathon. The signature waterfront course was adopted in 1999 and, with its wide, scenic route, paved the way for future expansion. Adroit marketing of the marathon as a more accessible alternative to New York, targeted primarily at the British and then the Mexican marathon markets, paid off, and foreign participation in the race began to emulate the diversity of the local population.

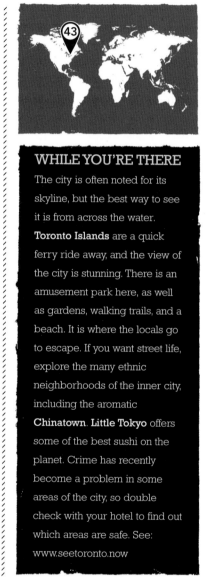

WHILE YOU'RE THERE

The city is often noted for its skyline, but the best way to see it is from across the water. **Toronto Islands** are a quick ferry ride away, and the view of the city is stunning. There is an amusement park here, as well as gardens, walking trails, and a beach. It is where the locals go to escape. If you want street life, explore the many ethnic neighborhoods of the inner city, including the aromatic **Chinatown**. **Little Tokyo** offers some of the best sushi on the planet. Crime has recently become a problem in some areas of the city, so double check with your hotel to find out which areas are safe. See: www.seetoronto.now

Above right: The CN Tower is a notable landmark that is clearly visible in this Toronto Waterfront Marathon.

Right: The balloon arches indicate that the finish line is not too far away.

In terms of performance, a Guinness World Record for "joggling" – the fringe sport of jogging and juggling at the same time – has been set by "The Joggler" when he ran the course in 3 hours and 7 minutes in 2005. And 72-year-old Ed Whitlock established a truly astonishing world age-best of 2:54. In more recent years the open age group has emulated Whitlock's effort, with the course record rapidly improving from 2:09 to 2:08 and now 2:07.

Both the marathon and half marathon start from the same spot in downtown Toronto. After 11 miles (18 km), half marathon runners branch off to the finish, while the marathon runners head on to make a tour of the eastern side of town. Peer across the water and you'll see the city skyline and one of the tallest buildings in the world, the CN Tower, before heading forward to the beaches district and then on to the finish.

RACE DETAILS

WHEN? October
WHEN TO APPLY: By January
HOW MANY TAKE PART? 15,000
DIFFICULTY RATING: 5/10
SPECIAL CONSIDERATIONS:
Unpredictable weather

CONTACT:
Scotiabank Toronto Waterfront Marathon
264 The Esplanade
Toronto, Ontario, M54 4J6, Canada

☎ +1 416 944 2765
🖥 www.torontowaterfrontmarathon.com

Niagara Falls International Marathon
USA & Canada

Few marathons start in one country and finish in another, but that is only half the claim to fame of the Niagara Falls International Marathon. The other half is the location of the finish line – within drifting distance of the spray arising from the Falls itself.

The idea for a marathon from Buffalo, New York, to Niagara Falls, Ontario, Canada, was conceived by a handful of musician runners from the Buffalo Philharmonic who regularly did a long run from the Peace Bridge in Fort Erie to the Rainbow Bridge in Niagara Falls, a distance of 18½ miles (30 km).

They called the run "bridge to bridge," recalls Jesse Kregal, a timpanist, who was part of the original group. Families would go along and meet the runners at the end for a picnic.

Left: This is a flat and fast course with plenty of organized on-course support.

Right: For most runners the scenic route and awe-inspiring finish are what makes this marathon magical.

Following page: The season is evident throughout this course, with the varied colors of the foliage.

RACE DETAILS

WHEN? October
WHEN TO APPLY: By March
HOW MANY TAKE PART? 1,000
DIFFICULTY RATING: 5/10
SPECIAL CONSIDERATIONS: Because of the parkway route, crowd support can be slim when you need it most. Bring your own fluids in case supplies run dry.

CONTACT:
Niagara Falls International Marathon
5300 Willmott Street
Niagara Falls, Ontario, Canada L2E 2A7
☎ +905 356 9460
✉ info@niagarafallsmarathon.com
🖥 www.niagarafallsmarathon.com

"Then we had the bright idea of having a race that would start some place in Buffalo and end at the Falls," said Kregal, a onetime race director. Runners gear up for the race in the unusual surroundings of an art gallery. The start of the race in Buffalo is low-key, as runners practically slink out of town to cross the Peace Bridge into Canada. There is a light sprinkling of support along the route, mainly from local people, but the main reward comes from the stunning natural scenery.

The idea of 1,000 runners streaming unchecked across the border at first seemed an insurmountable problem, but Canadian immigration was persuaded to pre-check and approve participants' passports. That done, the inaugural marathon was held on October 26, 1974, and the race has continued to attract runners in their thousands. This is largely due to the autumnal beauty of the scenery along roads that Winston Churchill called "the most stunning Sunday drive in the world."

For others, the highlight of the race comes early, as they cross from the US into Canada after about 5 miles (8 km). To the left is the vast expanse of Lake Erie, and to the right is the beginning of the Niagara River Parkway. In clear weather it is possible to see the plume of white mist rising from the Falls, 16¾ miles (27 km) downriver. The finish lies just 164 feet (50 m) from the Canadian Horseshoe Falls, a natural wonder that draws 14-million visitors a year.

Havana Marathon | Cuba

Like most of what is on show in the Cuban capital, the "Marabana" event may not be able to rival the bigger international marathons, but it offers an intimate glimpse into the character of the place. You will feel privileged to run alongside locals who make do without all the technological trappings that runners seem to find necessary elsewhere.

Going without energy gels or drinks and technological fabrics that "wick" your sweat away is quite usual here, so if you can't do without them, bring your own. It is how marathons used to be before the marketing people got to work, except that some people do not have running shoes either. In response, many regular runners from overseas bring a pair of old running shoes to donate to their unshod fellow competitors, in a true spirit of camaraderie.

The event can often seem a random and spontaneous affair, with even the registration process being put together just hours before the starting gun is fired. Often there's an olympic champion, such as Alberto Juantorena, Ana Quirot, or Javier Sotomayor, to wave the flag that begins the race.

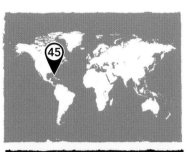

WHILE YOU'RE THERE

You can read all about the history of Cuba at the **Museo de la Revolución,** where the revolutionary ideals are set out and the story of the modern state is recorded. There is a loving shrine to **Che Guevara,** including locks of his hair and fragments of his socks. You cannot leave without taking a **tour of the city** in a '50s Cadillac – kept in working order. Stop at the **cigar factory,** too, to see how the country's world-famous cigars are made.

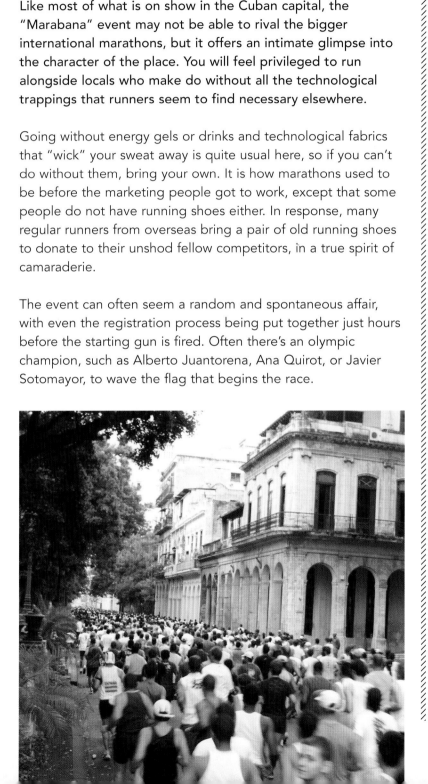

Left: The Havana Marathon consists of two laps of a city that has an old-world charm.

The course is two laps, and a half marathon is run at the same time over a single lap. Starting at Paseo del Prado, the run heads down toward the Malecón, a broad boulevard onto which waves of the Atlantic crash, splashing over the roadway and onto the runners. The route goes inland to the Raúl Diaz Sports Complex before turning back toward Havana Old Town, El Capitolio, and the Malecón, passing by the monumental public space and statue of the Plaza de la Revolución along the way.

Conditions can be hot and humid, but there are water and orange stations every 1½ miles (2–3 km). Havana is a mildly testing event topographically, but more challenging and infinitely more rewarding in cultural terms. The first 5½ miles (9 km) along the coast is flat before you turn inland, then the course becomes hilly for the remainder of the lap. On those grounds, it is all the more suitable for beginners keen for a running adventure.

Above: Havana is a UNESCO World Heritage city, and the marathon route takes full advantage of all it has to offer.

Right: The course of the marathon is not made exclusive to marathon runners.

RACE DETAILS

WHEN? November
WHEN TO APPLY: By March
HOW MANY TAKE PART? 3,000
DIFFICULTY RATING: 6/10
SPECIAL CONSIDERATIONS: Air quality
can be affected by traffic smoke.
Temperatures can reach 86°F (30°C).

CONTACT:

☎ +537 641 0911
✉ marabana@inder.cu
🖥 www.inder.cu/marabana

Chicago Marathon | USA

First held in 1977 as Mayor Daley's Marathon, this event became established as "America's Marathon" in the early 1980s. Britain's Steve Jones set a world record in 1984, grabbing the attention of elite runners looking for a fast course, but by 1987 uncertainties in sponsorship led to funds running low, and fewer elite runners took part. Although the race continued to be held annually, it had no sponsor in 1991–92, but then Lasalle Bank took up the title sponsorship and plowed in enough funding for the race organizers to be able to secure appearances by some of the world's best runners. Chicago then became a venue to rival London, New York, and Boston, as world records were set by Khalid Khannouchi in 1999, Catherine Ndereba in 2001, and Paula Radcliffe in 2002.

More than 4,200 runners turned out for the inaugural race in 1977, making the Chicago Marathon the largest in the world at the time. In recent years, it has been the fourth largest and seems poised to overtake London and Berlin.

WHILE YOU'RE THERE

After expending all those calories, explore the culinary delights of this city, from the pasta delights of **Little Italy** to indulging in a burger at the **Millennium Park Grill**. The Chicago Marathon is an occasion to experience the many great tastes of Chicago. Immediately following the race, runners can celebrate their accomplishment at the **27th Mile Post-Race Party** in Grant Park. All adult runners receive a complimentary 312 Urban Wheat Ale from Chicago's own Goose Island. See: www.gochicago.com

Left: The crowds never thin out on this mass-participation marathon.

Right: Downtown Chicago offers some great distractions to tiring runners.

Following page (top): Entertainment and goodwill are evident throughout this marathon course.

RACE DETAILS

WHEN? October
WHEN TO APPLY: By January
HOW MANY TAKE PART? 45,000
DIFFICULTY RATING: 4/10
SPECIAL CONSIDERATIONS:
Unpredictable climate can mean the weather can either be cold, windy, or sunny. Recent years have seen hot weather, but it is best to pack for any eventuality.

CONTACT:
Bank of America Chicago Marathon
135 S. LaSalle St., Suite 1160
MC: IL4-135-11-61
Chicago, IL 60603, USA
☎ +312 904 9800
✉ office@chicagomarathon.com
🖥 www.chicagomarathon.com

The course is flat, beginning in the city center and winding through all the distinctively different ethnic neighborhoods. Local residents make their presence felt at every stage of the course, vying to become the area offering the most enthusiastic support. Attractions include the male cheerleaders in Boystown, Fleet Feet's Elvis impersonator in Old Town, Old Street Pat's Church in the West Loop, the Mariachi band in Pilsen, and the dancing dragons in Chinatown.

The marathon route passes by several famous landmarks, including the 110-story Willis Tower (the tallest building in North America), the Chicago Theater on State Street, Lincoln Park Zoo, the Charles J. Hull House, and Wrigley Field.

The loop configuration of the course allows spectators to watch runners from more than one spot. With a downtown start and finish, runners and spectators alike can walk from their hotel to the start and back from the finish, avoiding the trouble of taking public transit.

The "windy city" in fact offers quite favorable conditions for running, as proved by the world records achieved here. October temperatures average a high of 61°F (16°C) and a low of 46°F (8°C).

Gran Maratón Pacifico | Mexico

The starting line of the Gran Maratón Pacifico in Mazatlán in Mexico's northwest looks more like a gathering of pilgrims than a race. There are young and old, people in wheelchairs and on crutches, blind people and the deaf, all taking part in an event that is a testimony to inclusiveness and the triumph of the human spirit over adversity.

Mazatlán, in the state of Sinaloa, is known as the Pearl of the Pacific for its beaches and its rich marine fauna. The weather in Mazatlán is hot, with an average daily high in December of 79°F (26°C).

The race was started in 1999 when the Pacific Brewery decided to mark its centenary by organizing an athletic event as part of a wider celebration of local culture. The route had one prerequisite, to take in Mazatlán Pier – the longest in the world and one that commands sweeping views of the Pacific Ocean.

The marathon is the main event, but there are races to suit everyone – 3 miles (5 km), 6 miles (10 km), a half marathon, and a 6-mile (10 km) event for wheelchair users. In its short history the race has drawn some of Mexico's best-known marathon runners, including Dionicio Cerón and Germán Silva.

WHILE YOU'RE THERE

There are beaches by day at an area called **The Golden Zone**, as well as a thriving nightlife. One way to see a different slice of life is to take a boat tour to **Stone Island**, with 12½ miles (20 km) of open beach lined with coconut palms. There are plenty of **thatched restaurants**, where you can soak up the relaxed atmosphere or have a well-earned beer while swaying in a hammock. There is also nightlife in town, with live music in bars such as **Joe's Oyster Bar**. See: www.mazatlan.travel

Left: There is a scenic course along the coast in Mazatlán, but beware, as it can it be windy and hot.

Far left (bottom): High-fives and street entertainment go hand-in-hand with the best marathons.

Top left: On marathon day, Chicago comes out in force to support the marathon participants.

Hydration is a concern in the high temperatures, so water stations are placed every 1½ miles (2 km) along the route, where the runners can find ice, water, and energy drinks. There are three "run-through" shower stations along the route – and a shower has never felt so reviving as it does here. The medical service is a major operation, with 10 specialist sports physicians and 120 paramedics on call for all runners.

The Festival of Light, of which the marathon forms part, is organized by the Pacific Brewery (one of their brews is "Pacific Light") and the Tres Islas Hoteliers' Association of Mazatlán. The festival offers one of the greatest firework displays in the Americas. There is also a pre-event carbo-loading feast, where around 10,000 guests tuck into plates of pasta, and of course the refreshing beer from the Pacific Brewery that gave rise to the whole marathon adventure.

Above: A wheelchair race runs alongside the main event at the Mazatlán Marathon.

Right: The race through the colonial town is open to all.

RACE DETAILS

WHEN? December
WHEN TO APPLY: May
HOW MANY TAKE PART? 6,500
DIFFICULTY RATING: 6/10
SPECIAL CONSIDERATIONS: Heat can be an issue. Stock up on energy drinks in case of scarcity on race day.

CONTACT:
Gran Maratón Pacifico
Plaza Maratones S.A de C. V.
Río Pánuco No. 157, Col Cuauhtémoc
CP 06500, Mexico D. F.
☎ +525 5280 1716
🖥 www.maraton.org

Big Sur International Marathon | USA

Big Sur is a 90-mile (145 km) stretch along the Californian coast, from the Carmel River in the north to the San Carpoforo Creek in the south. The Big Sur International Marathon started in 1986, when race founder Bill Burleigh stopped to ponder a simple road sign at the junction of Rio Road and the coastal Highway 101. As a Big Sur resident and runner he knew that running a marathon into the town of Carmel (former mayor: Clint Eastwood) along Big Sur, one of the most gorgeous stretches of coastline in the world, would be a surefire winner. The inaugural marathon drew a crowd of 1,800 and provided a spectacular backdrop of rolling hills, rugged Pacific coastline, and geological and meteorological forces that would daunt anyone without a marathon mentality.

The exposed nature of Big Sur means that every race day is a challenge. The first question is whether the earth will move; after all, this is the line of the San Andreas Fault. The second is whether the land will slip – that happened in 1998 and 2011 and involved some fancy footwork by Burleigh and his successor, Wally Kastner, to salvage a workable course. What the weather will bring is another question. Gale-force winds, hail, and thick fog are not unusual, although mild temperatures, clear blue skies, and even a gentle breeze from the south encouraging runners to the finish line are equally possible.

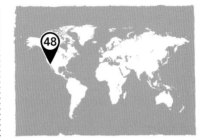

WHILE YOU'RE THERE

While you're there, there is no doubt that Big Sur is California's natural wonder, packed with national parks, beaches, and coastal walks. **Highway 101** helps you see the majority. Of all the beaches **Pfeiffer Beach** is the best-loved but charges a $5 entry fee to help keep it in pristine shape, although it is frequently ravaged by winds. More natural beauty abounds in **Los Padres National Forest** and **Point Lobos** for **whale watching**. The big metropolis of **San Francisco** awaits and is a 3-hour drive away.

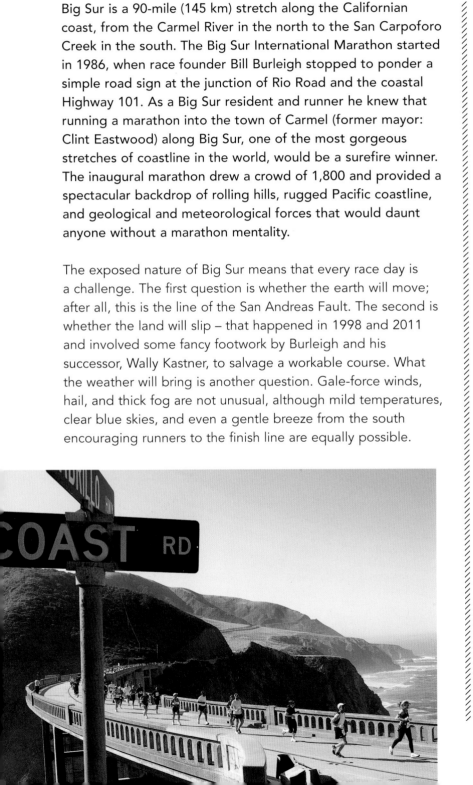

Left: Places in the Big Sur International Marathon sell out fast; this course is not the easiest, but it does have stunning views.

Mother Nature's mischief has never been enough to stop the marathon, but in 1995 floods destroyed the Carmel River Bridge just 650 feet (200 m) from the finish. A last-minute operation ensured the construction of a temporary structure to allow the show (or "presentation" in the organizers' words) to go on.

The course is unforgettably scenic, passing beneath the majestic redwoods of Big Sur and over gently gurgling streams during the first 5 miles (8 km). From there on it gets dramatic. There are mountains on the right-hand side, with green fields and wildflowers in the immediate foreground. On the left lies the Pacific Ocean, with its crashing waves and rocky cliffs. If runners look carefully they might be lucky enough to see whales and sea lions, condors, and wild turkeys.

Bill Burleigh obviously appreciated ironic juxtaposition and introduced an innovative marriage between classical music and wild nature. On the side of the road at the halfway point you will encounter a player at the keyboard of a grand piano.

Below: There are landmarks aplenty on this run, and if you are lucky you may see humpback whales.

RACE DETAILS

WHEN? April
WHEN TO APPLY: By April of the year before
HOW MANY TAKE PART? 4,500
DIFFICULTY RATING: 8/10
SPECIAL CONSIDERATIONS: Being exposed to the sea brings variable weather of wind, rain, and sun. Be prepared for all three in one race. Hills and inclines throughout. Excellent organization keeps the race together.

CONTACT:
Big Sur International Marathon
PO Box 222620
Carmel, CA 93922-2620, USA

☎ +8319 625 6226
✉ info@bsim.org
🖳 www.bsim.org/site3.aspx

World's Coolest |
The Poles

Antarctic Ice Marathon, Antarctica

The only race on mainland Antarctica and within the Antarctic Circle was first run in 2006 as a sister race to the North Pole Marathon, and at 10,000 euros it is almost as expensive to enter. The field has steadily grown, but a limit of 40 is currently imposed. The marathon route involves a 15½-mile (25 km) "outer" circuit followed by a 10½-mile (17.2 km) "inner" circuit. There is also a 62-mile (100 km) race involving four laps of the 15½-mile (25 km) circuit, and this is run on a different day than the marathon.

The marathon itself is run at 3,300 feet (1,000 m) altitude and against a stunning backdrop of mountains and hills. The underfoot conditions on this course sap the energy, although it is groomed and checked for

RACE DETAILS

WHEN? First week of April
WHEN TO APPLY: Two years in advance.
HOW MANY TAKE PART? 54
DIFFICULTY RATING: 9/10
SPECIAL CONSIDERATIONS: By no means your average marathon. −22°F (−30°C) temperatures and a 12,000 euro entry fee, you run on ice, not land.

CONTACT:
North Pole Marathon
Polar Running Adventures
2 Atlanta House
Dominick Street
Galway, Ireland
☎ +353 91 516 644
✉ rd@npmarathon.com
🖥 www.npmarathon.com

crevices before the race, which usually takes place in December. Competitors sometimes combine the trip with climbing Mount Vinson (the highest mountain in Antarctica) or flying onward to stand at the precise geographic South Pole. The temperature is typically between 14 and –4°F (–10 and –20°C) at its coldest. There is no wildlife here; in fact, there is no life at all – penguins can be found at the coast but do not venture into the forbidding interior of the Antarctic. The sense of remoteness is magnified during the race, as there is no sound except the wind and your own breathing.

North Pole Marathon

Make way for the James Bond school of marathons. Think about being dispatched by helicopter, running over ice, and traversing the domain of polar bears. The race may be "the world's coolest marathon," but it is also the world's costliest. The price of 12,000 euros does not even include the trip to the jumping-off point in Svaalbard, at 80° North. Even so, running this marathon is the least expensive way to visit the North Pole.

The challenge is to run on the frozen Arctic ice cap. The race date is governed each year by the establishment of a Russian camp, which is created by a specialist Russian logistics company

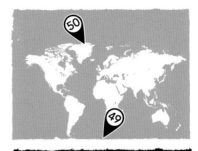

For many, just being in these extreme reaches of the world is an experience in itself. Unlike most marathon destinations, the terrain is desolate and unpredictable. Runners come here, not just to delight in having ventured so far, but to run long distance where few people have been before. To add to the novelty, there's 24 hours of daylight at both events. Celebrations run wild afterwards. For the North Pole Marathon there's a vodka party at the Pole after the race and many celebratory drinks on the athletes' return to Spitsbergen, Norway. For the Antarctic Ice Marathon, there's usually a big party in the dining tents after the race… and the nightlife in Punta Arenas is enjoyed both before and after the trip.

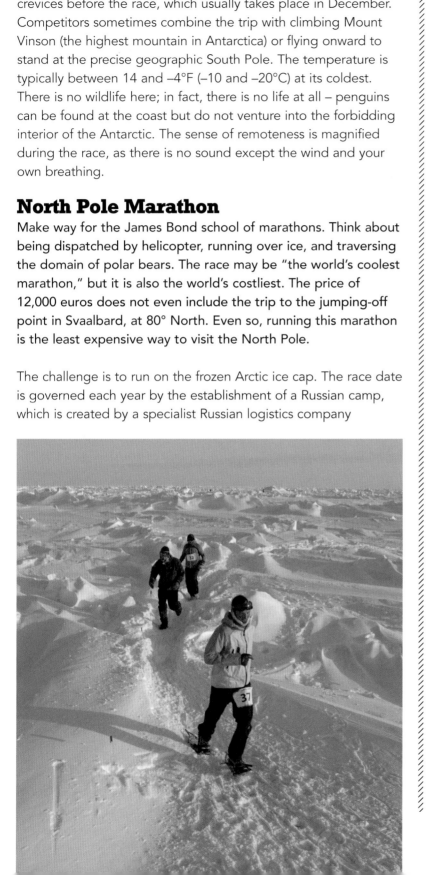

Left: The North Pole Marathon is an extreme, ultra-endurance event for those with astonishing fitness levels and a deep pocket.

Far left: This course is only appropriate for experienced runners.

airdropping a tractor and parachuting personnel onto the ice to construct a landing runway.

The underfoot conditions can be difficult in places as runners must negotiate small hillocks of ice known as "sastrugi" to complete the marathon. The course is well flagged and carefully arranged to avoid any breaks in the ice or "leads" that expose the ocean. There are 24 hours of daylight during the event, which is normally held at the end of the first week of April – the most likely temperature is 13°F (–25°C) with clear blue skies. Expect no crowd support, except for the few Russian personnel stationed at the camp. For safety reasons, the route is a multi-circuit course typically around 3 miles (5 km). Polar bears are a remote threat, and guns are kept on hand to deal with any such threat. The scenery is spectacular, with endless miles of ice and a sun that never sets. It is a surreal experience for those who take part.

Below: Camaraderie is strong among this small band of marathon runners.